Design, Construction & Modifications

A previous volume in this series, ShipCraft 11, was devoted to inter-war British destroyers of the broadly similar 'A' to 'I' classes, but concluded with the radically different 'Tribal' class. This one covers the succeeding classes, from the 'J's, which were entering service at the outbreak of the war, to the 'Battle's, which were just commissioning at its conclusion. Thus, the earlier title features the two-funnelled classes and this one their single-funnelled successors.

'J' AND 'K' CLASSES

The 'Tribal' class of 1935 were considered too large by some naval officers and the Admiralty's requirement for the next class was for smaller vessels but still with a powerful gun armament (HA/LA) and two sets of torpedo tubes (the 'Tribal's carried only one set). There was a great deal of discussion regarding the guns and the relative importance of LA and HA fire – 4in or 4.7in calibre, single or twin mountings and 40° or 70° elevation were all considered. Priority was given to surface engagements, hence the selection of the 4.7in gun with limited elevation (just 40°) but using a heavier 62lb shell (even though it was thought that a shortage of mountings would

require the first ships of the class to be fitted with at least two single mountings initially), and the pentad torpedo tubes.

One particular requirement was for a small silhouette and hence a single funnel was adopted, and much attention was paid to stability. The ships were to have longitudinal framing rather than transverse framing, a change from normal practice but one which had been used for one destroyer (*Ardent* built by Denny) before the First World War. There was also a lot of discussion regarding how many boilers were to be fitted, eventually two (which suited the single funnel) being selected.

The first sketch designs were submitted in August 1936 and, after some redrawing of the lines and a series of model tests, the final legend was submitted for approval in February 1937. Although completed building drawings were not available, tenders were requested almost immediately with the intention of placing orders by the end of March. The tenders were each for one 'J' class and one 'K' class vessel, the contracts for the 'J' class to be placed in March and those for the 'K' class in April. As for the preceding 'Tribal' class, the number of vessels was limited to just eight per flotilla with the leaders (*Jervis* and *Kelly*) being easily distinguished by the larger aft deckhouse and hence insufficient

Below: HMS *Jersey* on builders' trials (note the J S White flag at the stern) in April 1939. The visible crew are civilians and some of the equipment – notably the rangefinder – is yet to be fitted. (*National Maritime Museum N11333*)

Opposite: One of the 4in-armed 'L' class, *Lance* is seen entering Grand Harbour, Valletta early in 1942. Close range AA defence has been improved by the addition of two single 20mm Oerlikons, one each side of the searchlight platform between the torpedo tubes. The dark structure beneath the fore yardarm is the HF/DF hut. While at Malta the ship was bombed in dry dock in April and eventually declared a constructive total loss.

Below: This photograph of HMS *Kandahar* was taken at Alexandria during 1941. The aft gun is stowed facing forwards and she carries two sets of torpedo tubes. (*National Maritime Museum N31759*)

room on the quarterdeck to fit the Two Speed Destroyer Sweep (TSDS) gear. TSDS was not fitted to any of the 'K' class. The building drawings were formally approved in April and John Brown were given the task of laying off the vessels' lines.

The aft gun mounting ('X' mounting) was initially installed to be stowed facing forwards, hence giving a 20° blind arc aft, but this was later reversed. The ships were intended to protect themselves against air attack, primarily with a quadruple 2pdr mounting fitted aft of the funnel where it had wide firing arcs, particularly astern, and with quadruple 0.5in machine guns mounted on the bridge wings protecting the forward arcs. Gun control was provided by the Director Control Tower (DCT) which transmitted both elevation and bearing signals to pointers on the mountings for the operators (layer and trainer) to follow, firing being by the director layer when ordered. Although the DCT had been modified to accept AA fire control instruments, it proved unsuitable for AA engagements and was only used for surface combat. The rangefinder was sited abaft the DCT and later carried a Type 285 radar antenna.

The torpedo tubes could train on either beam and were fired electrically from the bridge. As well as the TSDS, the vessels carried two depth charge throwers and a rack for 20 depth charges. There was also a 44in searchlight fitted amidships and the ships were fitted with a light tripod mast. Both leaders, *Jervis* and *Kelly*, were to be fitted with D/F equipment. These vessels were considered to be very seaworthy but some problems were experienced with spray over the bridge and 'B' gun mounting. A number of captains also expressed reservations regarding the number and types of boats carried. Even though these were smaller vessels than the 'Tribal's, being

shorter and carrying two less guns but an additional set of torpedo tubes, they were no less complex and cost was increased.

In May 1940 pennant numbers of the 'J' and 'K' classes were changed, the digits remaining the same but the preceding letter ('flag superior') changing from 'F' to 'G'. Degaussing equipment was fitted in the later ships while they were under construction and as the opportunities arose for the earlier vessels (*eg Janus* in January 1940, *Jervis* and *Jupiter* in February, *Jaguar* in October and *Kingston* in April 1940).

As they became available radars Types 286, 285 and 252 were fitted, as were direction finding equipments FH3 (HF/DF) and FM7 (MF/DF). *Javelin* received Type 286 (a modified RAF set) in June 1940 and *Jervis* received Type 285 in October 1942 whilst at Alexandria. *Nestor* received Type 285 from her builders in April 1941, shortly after her completion. *Janus* was fitted with HF/DF equipment in December 1943.

The four ships of the first two classes that survived the war (*Jervis*, *Javelin*, *Kelvin* and *Kimberley*) were fitted with lattice masts to support various antennas, *Jervis* and *Kelvin* receiving radar Type 271, *Javelin* receiving Type 272 and *Kimberley* Type 276. *Jervis* had her equipment fitted whilst in Belfast in late 1944/early 1945. Lattice masts were also fitted to the 'N' class repeats *Napier*, *Nizam*, *Norseman* and *Norman*, this last also having a pole mast aft to carry the HF/DF antenna.

AA protection was enhanced by the fitting of 20mm Oerlikon mountings in lieu of the bridge wing machine guns, some vessels receiving these while still under construction and before completion. Additional mountings were also added on both sides of the searchlight and, in some cases, on the quarterdeck. Initially single mountings were fitted but the majority were

later replaced by twin mountings. *Jupiter* received some in July 1941 and *Jervis* had two fitted in November 1942. *Napier* received an additional pair in September 1941 and yet another pair in April 1942, whilst at Bombay. For a period (late 1941/1942), a single 4in AA gun replaced the aft set of torpedo tubes.

'L' AND 'M' CLASSES

The main requirement for the next class of destroyers was higher speed (in order to maintain a reasonable margin over the increasing speed of capital ships) and weatherproof gun mountings. The latter would increase weight significantly, despite a reduction in the number of torpedoes, and therefore much higher power would be required to increase speed significantly.

The resulting sketch design submitted in October 1937 had three twin 4.7in mountings with 50° elevation, enhanced AA gun armament but only quadruple torpedo tubes and a slight increase in speed – basically, a slightly enlarged and improved 'J' class. Again, contractors were invited to inspect preliminary drawings in order to provide tenders, as the completed build drawings were not available. Invitations to tender were sent out at the beginning of March 1938, with responses required by the 18th and the letters of acceptance were issued by the end of the month. The Admiralty formerly accepted the design in April and the contracts were confirmed in August.

As well as the increase in elevation and the weatherproof housings of the three primary gun mountings, the barrels could be elevated independently. The DCT was to be used for both LA and HA engagements and to include the rangefinder, with its Type 285 radar. With one officer on the bridge, the DCT was manned by one officer and five ratings with eight other ratings below in the transmitting station.

In addition to the six primary guns, the design called for AA protection to be enhanced by the fitting of two quadruple 2pdr mountings with space for a director

when a suitable system became available. The final design had just one quadruple 2pdr mounting plus two 20mm Oerlikon guns and quadruple 0.5in machine guns. The latter were replaced with 20mm guns and more 20mm mountings were added, two on the quarterdeck and one each side of the searchlight position.

A shortage of the primary guns resulted in a decision in July 1940 to fit four of the 'L' class (*Lance*, *Larne*, *Legion* and *Lively*) with eight 4in guns in four mountings (requiring a longer aft superstructure), but these vessels were to be fitted with two sets of torpedo tubes. The aft torpedo tubes were fitted with a protected position for the trainer and the forward set received a spray shield, an improvement that was also fitted to both 'J' and 'K' class vessels. Complement was to be 190, slightly lower than that for the 'J' and 'K classes, with the AA ships having 221 and the leader, *Laforey*, 224.

The ships which were fitted with the 4.7in mountings (ie *Laforey*, *Lightning*, *Lookout* and *Loyal* and all the 'M' class) included the option of installing a single 4in HA mounting, to enhance the AA defence, in lieu of the aft set of torpedoes. All completed with the 4in gun in lieu of the torpedo tubes, but the torpedo tubes were installed later when the 4in gun was removed.

Below: HMS *Lookout* in 1942 carries radar Type 291 on the foremast with Type 285 on the DCT. A 4in HA gun replaces the aft torpedo tubes and single 20mm mountings have been fitted on the bridge wings and abreast the searchlight, but on the quarterdeck (where others of the class carried single Oerlikons) there are two twin 0.5in machine guns in Mk V powered mountings of the kind normally carried by MTBs.

Right: This overhead view of *Nepal* in 1942 illustrates the layout of the class. She was completed with a 4in HA gun in place of the after bank of torpedo tubes, and the light AA armament here comprises six single 20mm Oerlikons: two in the bridge wings, two abreast the searchlight platform and two on the quarterdeck. The camouflage appears to be a two-colour Admiralty Disruptive scheme, probably in MS1 and MS4. *Nepal* was the only member of the class to be RN-manned for the whole of the war, the remainder being transferred to, or manned by, the Polish, Dutch and Australian Navies.

Below: HMS *Marne* in April 1946, wearing her paying-off pendant. She has a plain grey hull and displays the flotilla number 3, a system that replaced the previous funnel bands. Unlike some ships of the class, she did not have a pole mast aft and consequently carried her Type 291 aerial at the fore topmast head. The Oerlikons in the bridge wings and abreast the searchlight platform are in twin powered mountings. *(National Museum of the Royal Navy)*

During the construction of these vessels, new radar and other electronic equipment began to make a significant appearance and so *Lance* and *Lively* were fitted with Type 286M at the masthead and *Gurkha* (ex-*Larne*) and *Legion* were fitted with a special HF/DF outfit. Type 290 was fitted in lieu of Type 286 in all the 'M' class except *Milne* (leader). The ASW armament was also increased by the addition of a second depth charge rail whilst retaining the two depth charge throwers.

In February 1941 *Lance* carried out successful trials of modified Radar Type 286M, using a rotating antenna instead of fixed aerial array. The new antenna was then put into production and, when fitted, the modified RAF Air/Surface outfit became Radar Type 286P which was far more suitable for ship use. *Lively* was fitted with HF/DF Outfit FH3, as was *Lookout*, and, during work-up took part in trials of a modified Type 271 radar which was later put into production as Type 273 and replaced the earlier centimetric Type 271 to provide surface cover.

Lookout, the only surviving member of the 'L' class, received a lattice mast, as did the surviving members of the 'M' class, except *Musketeer*. The 'M' class vessels all carried radar Type 272 on the lattice mast and it was in the second half of 1943, that *Marne* was fitted with her radar. *Musketeer* retained Type 291 at her masthead and had Type 271 fitted amidships in lieu of her searchlight. Like *Norman*, *Matchless* had a pole mast aft to carry the HF/DF antenna.

The AA armament was enhanced in similar ways to the previous ships, the 4in AA gun being carried in lieu of the aft set of torpedo tubes for a while and the smaller calibre guns being changed to 20mm and increased in number, using twin mountings.

'N' CLASS

In March 1939 it was decided that in order to hasten entry into service, the next class would be repeats of the 'K' class but TSDS would be fitted. There were other detail changes of a minor nature and a 4in AA gun was initially fitted in lieu of the aft set of torpedo tubes, as in the 'L' and 'M' classes.

Tenders were provisionally accepted in April 1939 but treaty limitations forbade the laying of any keels until the end of July. Formal contract acceptance was not given until January 1940. Delays in the availability of fire control equipment held up the delivery of the ships and 20mm Oerlikon mountings were fitted in lieu of the 0.5in machine guns as they became available.

The ships of the 'N' class that served with the British Pacific Fleet underwent changes to their pennant numbers in March 1945, *Napier* becoming D13, *Nepal* becoming D14, *Nizam* D15 and *Norman* D16.

Left: After the big destroyers of the 'J' to 'N' classes, there was a return to moderate dimensions for what became known as the Intermediate design. This became the 'O' and 'P' flotillas which were produced in two versions, the more conventional mounting four 4.7in guns, as shown in this July 1942 view of *Onslaught* . The director was a stopgap Mk V** as fitted in 'Hunt' class escort destroyers; it sits low on the bridge to minimise the mechanical connection to the Transmitting Station below but carried the usual Type 285 aerials. As with so many fleet destroyers a 4in HA replaced the after torpedo tubes and AA armament was completed by a quad 2pdr pom-pom and four single 20mm. The ship wears a pale two-tone Western Approaches camouflage.

Below: HMS *Nepal* in May 1942 mounts a 4in HA gun in lieu of the aft bank of torpedo tubes and six single 20mm guns (sided in the bridge wings, abreast the searchlight platform and on the quarterdeck). The rangefinder is fitted with radar Type 285 and Type 291 is carried on the foremast. (*National Maritime Museum N11858*)

'O' AND 'P' CLASSES

The first sketch designs for the 1st War Emergency Flotilla or 'O' class were submitted in January 1939 and revised in May, receiving approval in December. Concerns had been expressed regarding the increasing cost and production time of destroyers and hence this class were to be simpler, quicker to produce and cheaper than the preceding classes. Main armament was reduced to four single mountings, as it had been in the inter-war 'A' to 'I' classes. Orders for the 1st Flotilla were placed in September 1939 with those for the 2nd Flotilla (or 'P' class) following in October.

The main role was still considered to be surface engagement with only a limited regard for aircraft attacks. The guns were to be hand worked with a maximum elevation of 40° and to fire a 50lb projectile. Two sets of quadruple torpedo tubes were to be fitted but with provision to replace the aft set with a 4in HA mounting. Close range defence was to be provided by a quadruple 2pdr mounting (retained in the following 'P','Q' and 'R' classes also) and eight 0.5in machine guns in two quadruple mountings.

ASW armament was to consist of two depth charge throwers and two rails but in May 1941 approval was given to increase to four throwers, with an associated increase in the number of depth charges carried. Asdic Type 128A was to be fitted and it was expected this would operate satisfactorily with shaft speeds up to 200rpm.

Although the hull was smaller than the preceding classes, in order to simplify construction machinery was to be as in the 'J' class. Other minor changes were incorporated in an attempt to reduce both cost and production times.

Difficulties were experienced with the supply of 4.7in mountings; early war experience highlighted the threat from aircraft; and a significant number of minelayers were lost early in the war. In March 1941, therefore, the Controller gave instructions to convert four of the 'O' class to include a minelaying capability, conversion to this role to be possible in less than 48 hours. *Opportune, Orwell, Obdurate* and *Obedient* were to be fitted with four 4in HA/LA mountings instead of the 4.7in guns. A maximum load of 60 mines could be carried by replacing the torpedo tubes and 'Y' gun, and the two depth charge throwers were relocated to make space for the minelaying rails.

The continuing problems with gun

supply led to the 'P' class also being constructed with either four 4in mountings or five if one set of torpedo tubes was landed. In order to maintain a consistent calibre of primary armament for each flotilla, *Onslow* and *Pakenham*, and *Onslaught* and *Pathfinder* were exchanged and renamed. The various changes included in the design led to concerns about stability and so measures were taken to reduce topweight where possible. These included lowering the height of the funnel by four feet and reducing deck head height.

In November 1941 it was decided to add two additional 0.5in mountings on the signal deck but by the time the ships were completed most of the 0.5in mountings had been replaced by 20mm weapons. Radars Types 271, 285 and 286 (at the masthead) were also added, as was MF/DF equipment. The DCT was suitable for both HA and LA engagements. *Offa* received a lattice mast in February 1943, *Onslow* in March of the same year and *Onslaught* in August. *Onslow* was fitted with radar Type 272 at the same time, *Offa* having received hers previously in February. As well as Type 272, *Onslow* also received an HF/DF set on a pole mast aft. In April 1942 *Pathfinder* had also been fitted with DF equipment.

Although the 4in AA mounting was landed and the aft set of torpedo tubes replaced, close-range defence was generally increased either by the installation of additional 20mm mountings or by replacing the single mountings with twins. At the end of 1944/early 1945, *Petard* had work carried out which included the replacement of single 4in mountings in 'B' and 'X' positions by twin mountings and 'A' mounting was removed. A lattice design foremast was also fitted to suit the new radar aerial fit.

Both *Oribi* and *Onslow* completed with quadruple 0.5in machine gun mountings in the bridge wings and two additional 20mm mountings were fitted on the searchlight platform shortly afterwards, at the same time as the 0.5in mountings were replaced with 20mm mountings. *Offa* had the additional 20mm mountings on her searchlight platform when completed and the 0.5in bridge wing mountings were replaced early in 1942. *Onslaught* completed with four 20mm mountings but later had the mountings on the searchlight platform replaced with twin mountings, as did *Offa* and *Onslow* in mid-1943. Those ships intended as minelayers (except *Obdurate*) completed with four 20mm mountings (located in the bridge wings and on the upper deck) and 0.5in mountings on the searchlight platform. The bridge wing mountings were replaced with twins during 1943/44.

Being completed a little later, the 'P' class all received four 20mm mountings, except for *Petard* and *Porcupine* which initially had two 20mm mountings and two quadruple 0.5in mountings. *Pathfinder* and *Penn* later had the bridge wing mountings replaced with twins and *Paladin* received the same upgrade to the mountings on the searchlight platform. *Petard* was refitted with twin 4in Mk XIX mountings in 'B' and 'X' positions. At that time she had four 20mm mountings on the searchlight platform and two in the bridge wings.

'Q' AND 'R' CLASSES

The sketch design for the 3rd Emergency Flotilla ('Q' class) was initially approved in February 1940 and final approval was received in May. Orders were placed in March 1940. These vessels retained the main armament of the earlier 'O' class but had slightly larger dimensions, hence giving an increased margin. When approved, the design included a 4in HA gun in place of the aft torpedo tubes but two sets of torpedo tubes were fitted when the ships completed.

Separate directors were mounted for HA and LA engagements and the ships carried two DC throwers and three DC racks. Normal stowage was for 45 depth charges but this could be increased to 120, together with six DC throwers if the aft gun was removed. The aft gun had to be removed also if TSDS was to be carried. The leader, *Quilliam*, had a wider aft superstructure in order to accommodate the additional staff.

An additional pair of 20mm guns were added abreast the searchlight and the HA DCT was fitted with Type 285 for ranging purposes and Type 290 was carried at the masthead. All completed with six single 20mm mountings but the majority later received twin mountings in the bridge wings.

Both *Queenborough* and *Quail* had their bridge wing mountings replaced by twin 20mm mountings, and *Quality* and *Quail* had four 20mm guns on the searchlight platform. *Quality* also had a Type 272 radar fitted between the two sets of torpedo tubes.

In late 1944/early 1945 *Quilliam*, *Quadrant*, *Quality*, *Queenborough* and *Quiberon* had their pennant numbers for visual signalling purposes changed to D22, D14, D18, D19 and D20, respectively, to conform to US Navy signal address identity for destroyers.

The 'R' class were virtually repeats of the 'Q' class but with minor changes, the main one being a reorganisation of the accommodation to bring officers from aft to amidships. Orders for these ships were placed in April 1940 but construction was delayed because of the high workload of repairs on other destroyers. The number of DC throwers was increased to four but the number of racks reduced to two. Radars Types 285 and 290 were carried as in the 'Q' class.

Roebuck and *Rocket* completed with twin 20mm mountings in the bridge wings, an upgrade that was later applied to the entire class. The four midships 20mm mountings were replaced by a single 40mm mounting in mid-1945 on both *Rapid* and *Rocket*.

Above: HMS *Quickmatch* in August 1942. Fire control in this and the subsequent classes down to the 'V's was through a separate DCT (for surface fire) and Mk II or II(W) rangefinder director for HA fire, although the latter also functioned as a rangefinder in surface mode; the rangefinder director carries Type 285 gunnery radar. There is a MF/DF (Medium Frequency Direction Finder) aerial carried on a bracket on the bridge front. *(US National Archives via Roger Torgeson)*

Left: HMS *Rapid* in August 1946 displays various changes to her radar outfit and the enhancement of her AA defence. The most striking alteration is the lattice foremast which now carries a Type 293 target indicating radar on the platform and a HF/DF antenna at the head of the topmast; the Type 291 has been moved to the top of a pole mainmast. All the AA weapons are under canvas so it is not easy to identify them, but by this date the ship had supposedly replaced her four single 20mm with four single 40mm Bofors, retaining twin 20mm in the bridge wings. *(National Museum of the Royal Navy)*

'S', 'T', 'U', 'V' AND 'W' CLASSES

In the early war years the number of destroyers being lost to air attacks caused much concern and so defence against this threat was a major consideration in the design of the next class of destroyers. The elevation of the 4.7in mountings was increased to a maximum of 55° – not sufficient for defence against dive bombers but adequate for most other types of air attack. Orders were placed in January 1941.

Following evaluation of the 40mm Hazemeyer mounting fitted to the Dutch destroyer *Van der Zaan* in mid-1940, three proposals were considered for the close range armament. *Scorpion* retained the quadruple 2pdr mounting but the others were fitted with a twin 40mm gun, mounted between the two sets of torpedo tubes, rather than just aft of the funnel, in order to increase the firing arc. Twin, rather than single, 20mm mountings were also included, two on the bridge wings and two aft of the funnel. *Swift* and *Savage* completed with two additional twin 20mm mountings on the 40mm platform, the latter also receiving two single 20mm mountings on the forward shelter deck during 1944. During 1945 *Saumarez* had all her 20mm mountings removed and replaced by four single 40mm mountings.

Saumarez, *Scorpion*, *Savage* and *Scourge* were fitted with a tripod mast forward and a lattice mast for HF/DF aft (not *Savage*). The later units were fitted with lattice masts carrying radar Type 272 and HF/DF, the aft mast being replaced by just a pole. The HA DCT carried Type 285 and the twin 40mm mountings were fitted with Type 282. Radar Type 290 was to be provided as a warning set.

The shape of the bow was changed in order to reduce spray, which resulted in a slight increase in overall length. The 'S' class was capable of carrying TSDS but all had four DC throwers and two DC rails fitted. The office for asdic Type 144 was increased in size.

Savage was used to experiment with a twin 4.5in HA (80°) mounting forward. In order to maintain consistency in calibre, single 4.5in mountings (55° elevation) were fitted aft. These two types of mounting acted as prototypes for those carried by the 'Battle' class and by the 'Z' and 'C' classes respectively. *Savage* was fitted with a tripod mast carrying radar Type 291 and radar Type 271 was fitted amidships but there was no mainmast.

The 'T' class, orders for which were placed in March 1941, were similarly fitted for TSDS but carried four depth charge throwers and two rails. These ships were not fitted for Arctic service, as had been the preceding 'S' class. *Tumult* initially carried two fixed torpedo tubes, angled out from the centreline, instead of the normal forward trainable bank but these were soon replaced.

Troubridge, *Tumult*, *Tuscan* and *Tyrian* had tripod foremasts carrying radar Type 291. Type 285 was fitted to the HA DCT. These four ships initially had ten 20mm guns on four twin (in the bridge wings and abaft the funnel) and two single mountings (amidships). *Troubridge* was also fitted with a lattice mast aft for HF/DF and *Tumult* had radar Type 271 amidships.

Teazer, *Tenacious*, *Termagant* and *Terpsichore* were built with lattice foremasts carrying both Type 272 and HF/DF and a pole mast carrying Type 291 aft. Apart from *Terpsichore* (six twin 20mm mountings), they were fitted with a twin 40mm mounting, between the torpedo tubes, and four twin 20mm mountings. In 1945 *Troubridge*, *Termagant* and *Tuscan* each received a single 40mm Mk III mounting in lieu of the searchlight and four 40mm mountings in the bridge wings and abaft the funnel, the 20mm mountings being removed. A single 40mm mounting was also fitted instead of the twin mounting on *Termagant*. At a similar time, *Tumult* had her 20mm mountings removed and received three single 40mm mountings abaft the funnel and a pom-pom in each bridge wing. *Tyrian* was fitted with two 40mm mountings abaft the funnel and twin 20mm mountings in the bridge wings.

In November 1943 *Tuscan* carried out sea trials for the newly developed surface warning radar Type 276. In the middle of 1945 the 'T' class had their pennant numbers changed to conform to the US Navy system of identity for destroyers: *Troubridge* became D49, *Tumult* became D50, *Terpsichore* became D33, *Tenacious*

Right: HMS *Savage* in 1943. This ship was the testbed for two new 4.5in mountings, the twin BD Mk IV with 80° elevation used in the 'Battles's and the single Mk V which went to sea in the 'Z' and 'C' classes. The 4.5in was to become the standard calibre for surface escorts postwar. The ship also carries a Type 271 surface search radar in place of the Hazemeyer mounting amidships, the light AA comprising six twin 20mm mountings. *(Naval Photograph Club)*

Left: Like *Savage*, *Swift* was also completed without a Hazemeyer mounting but relied on six twin 20mm for AA defence. In her case the surface search radar, Type 272 (an improved 271), was mounted on the platform of a lattice mast (the original reason for introducing them), but they were not sufficiently rigid and vibration reduced the effectiveness of the radar.

became D23, *Teazer* became D45, *Tuscan* became D51, *Tyrian* became D52 and *Termagant* became D47.

The 'U' class utilised spare quintuple torpedo tubes, with the centre tube removed. TSDS was not a requirement but they retained four DC throwers and two rails. Apart from *Grenville* (leader) and *Ulster* which received tripod masts, the class were fitted with short lattice masts carrying radar Type 271, the aforementioned being fitted later with taller lattice masts carrying Type 276, Type 291 and HF/DF. In October to December 1944 *Ulster* received a new design of lattice foremast fitted in place of earlier tripod type, radar Type 276 for surface warning was replaced with Type 242 and the associated IFF outfit fitted in place of the Type 272 fitted during build. Some ships in the flotilla had fire control radar Type 282 fitted for close range armament and IFF equipment was also fitted for Type 291 radar.

A shortage of twin 40mm mountings resulted in *Ulysses* completing with a quadruple 2pdr mounting and *Undine* and *Urchin* receiving two twin 20mm mountings in lieu. In 1945 *Grenville*, *Ulysses*, *Ursa*, *Undine* and *Urchin* were fitted with a single 40mm mounting Mk III in lieu of the searchlight and had four 40mm 'Boffins' (in effect, a single Bofors barrel on the body of the twin Oerlikon mount) fitted on the bridge wings and abaft the funnel. *Urania* received four Mk III 40mm mountings in place of the twin 20mm mountings.

As for the 'T' class, the 'U' class also received new pennant numbers in the middle of 1945, *Urania* becoming D27, *Ulster* D23, *Grenville* D11, *Ursa* D29, *Undine* D26, *Undaunted* D25, *Ulysses* D24 and *Urchin* D28.

Apart from *Venus*, which received a tripod mast, the 'V' class were completed with the same short lattice mast with radar Type 276 and HF/DF. They also carried a short pole mast aft with Type 291. *Vigilant* differed by carrying Type 291 on her foremast and having a short lattice mast for HF/DF equipment aft. *Volage* received a quadruple 2pdr mounting but the others all carried a twin 40mm mounting, with radar Type 282. Radar Type 285 was fitted to the HA DCT. The 'V' class were fitted for Arctic service.

In April to June 1945 *Volage* received an additional warning radar Type 291 and an improved submarine detection set (A/S

Left: The manufacture of the complex Hazemeyer mounting could not keep pace with demand so a number of the mid-war destroyers completed without one, or with a quad pom-pom as a substitute. The newly completed HMS *Terpsichore* seen here in January 1944 had neither and relied on twelve 20mm Oerlikons (6 x 2, sided in bridge wings, abaft funnel and amidships) for AA defence, although the Hazemeyer was installed later. *(By courtesy of David Hobbs)*

Type 147B), as well as a radio equipment for direction finding of wireless communication transmissions. *Volage* completed with a quadruple 2pdr pom-pom mounting in place of the twin 40mm mounting and during 1945 a number of modifications were carried out, *Venus* and *Vigilant* receiving four single Mk III 40mm mountings in place of their twin 20mm mountings, *Verulam* having her twin 20mm mountings abaft the funnel replaced with 40mm mountings Mk III and two additional Mk III mountings added abreast the mainmast. *Volage* also received four Mk III mountings and all her 20mm mountings were removed.

The 'W' class were completed with tall lattice masts, carrying radar Type 272 and HF/DF, and short pole masts aft, carrying radar Type 291. The separate DCTs were replaced by a single unit which carried Type 285. *Wessex* and *Whelp* initially carried a quadruple 2pdr mounting in lieu of the twin 40mm mounting, but with the ever increasing need for enhanced AA defence, the majority of ships acquired heavier armament whenever possible. *Kempenfelt*, *Wager*, *Wessex* and *Whelp* shipped a 40mm gun in lieu of the searchlight, *Wager* also receiving four 'Boffins' instead of twin 20mm mount-

ings. *Wakeful* had three Mk III mountings abaft the funnel and *Wizard*, two.

The 'W' class also received new pennant numbers, *Kempenfelt* becoming D12, *Whelp* D33, *Wrangler* D36, *Wakeful* D31, *Wizard* D35, *Whirlwind* D34, *Wessex* D32 and *Wager* D30.

The orders for the 'U' class were placed in June 1941, those for the 'V' class in September and those for the 'W' class in December.

'Z', 'CA', 'CH', 'CO' AND 'CR' CLASSES

Orders for the 'Z' class were placed in February 1942. This and the following classes introduced the new 4.5in Mk IV gun on Mk V mountings, which were fitted with remote power control (RPC) and could therefore automatically follow the DCT in both elevation and training. The new DCT Mk VI was selected but it was not until the 'Ch' class that equipment production could match construction timescales, so a stopgap director, known as the Mk I Type K, was installed in the first two flotillas.

Short lattice masts were fitted in *Myngs* (leader), *Zambesi* and *Zest* while the rest of the 'Z' class had the taller lattice masts.

Left: HMS *Kempenfelt*, the 'W' class leader. A tradition grew up in the Royal Navy of naming destroyer leaders after famous naval officers – not the headline-making admirals who were celebrated by larger ships, but lesser lights whose exploits were still worthy of commemoration. If at all possible, the leader shared the same initial as the rest of the flotilla (which worked from *Jervis* to *Troubridge*) but this became difficult towards the end of the alphabet and it was abandoned for the 'U' to 'Z' classes whose leaders were, respectively, *Grenville*, *Hardy*, *Kempenfelt* and *Myngs*.

Radar Type 293 was fitted to all. The A/S equipment comprised four depth charge throwers and two rails, and was the same for the 'Ca' class.

In order to reduce the effect of the heavier DCT, single 20mm mountings were to be fitted either side of the searchlight (except in *Zambesi* which had twins) with twin 20mm mountings in the bridge wings, this being in addition to the two 40mm mountings. Because of continuing problems with supply, *Zenith* was completed with single 2pdr mountings in place of all the 20mm mountings, *Myngs* had 2pdr mountings fitted on the bridge wings and *Zephyr* had them on either side of the searchlight. To further enhance the close range defence, *Myngs* was also fitted with a 40mm mounting in lieu of the searchlight.

Orders for what was to become the 'Ca' class were placed in February 1942. A wide variety of names were allocated to the ships when ordered (*eg Pellew, Swallow* and *Ranger*) but, having transferred many of the previous 'C' class to Canada, the Admiralty decided to replace them with a new 'C' class.

Supply difficulties continued for both the DCT and the smaller calibre weapons and so the close range armament varied upon completion although all received their design equipments in due course. Many of the 'Ca' class received a Mk III(W) DCT, *Caprice* received quadruple 2pdr mountings in lieu of the 40mm mountings, *Caesar* had single 2pdr mountings and *Cassandra* single 20mm mountings in the bridge wings. When upgraded, *Caprice, Cassandra* and *Cavendish* received twin 20mm mountings instead of single mountings either side of the searchlight.

The orders for the 'Ch' class were placed in July 1942. These ships were actually fitted with the Mk VI DCT with radar Type 275, which was heavier than in previous classes, resulting in the need to omit the forward bank of torpedo tubes, which, like the 4.5in guns, were to be fitted with RPC, to compensate. Further compensation was made by fitting single 20mm mounts on the bridge wings with just four twin mountings elsewhere.

The final outfit was to be four 40mm guns (two single mounts aft of the funnel with a twin mount amidships) and two single 20mm mounts in the bridge wings but not all ships received these by the time of completion. *Chaplet* and *Charity* were completed with single 2pdr mountings aft of the funnel, *Childers* had no guns in these positions and *Chequers* and *Cheviot* had

Left: Although they looked very similar to the preceding flotillas, the 'Z' class introduced the important innovation of the 4.5in Mk IV gun, conceived as a dual purpose weapon. It was difficult to tell from its predecessor because its Mk V mounting was virtually identical to the Mk XXII of the earlier 4.7in and allowed the same 55° elevation. It was originally intended to fit them with a new director and remote power control (RPC) but the development of what became the Mk VI was protracted and the 'Z' class were fitted with an interim design known as the Mk I Type K, or K Tower. This was a complex stabilised unit that proved difficult to maintain and production problems meant some of the class commissioning without a director. This is HMS *Zephyr* in December 1945 with the K Tower in place.

Right: The 'Ca' flotilla were effectively repeats of the 'Z' class, but they seem to have suffered rather more from shortages of light weaponry. *Caesar*, seen her in 1945, seems to be missing her Hazemeyer amidships (actually, it is turned away from the viewer showing off the screen that was fitted on the back of the mounting in its later versions), there is a single 40mm Bofors where the searchlight was located in earlier classes, while the bridge wing weapon is a single 2pdr pom-pom; there are no other light AA guns.

twin 20mm mountings in the bridge wings and aft of the funnel.

Radar Type 282 was carried on the twin 40mm mountings with Type 293 on the foremast and Type 291 on a pole mast aft. Because of weight problems, anti-submarine weapons were limited to two depth charge throwers and two racks, with just 35 depth charges.

The 'Co' and 'Cr' classes, ordered in July and September 1942 respectively, were intended as repeats of the 'Ch' class but, once again, limitations in the availability of light weapons resulted in *Comet* completing with 2pdr mountings in the bridge wings and aft of the funnel whilst *Constance* and *Cossack* had the same mountings aft of the funnel. *Contest* was the first destroyer of all-welded construction.

'BATTLE' CLASS (FIRST GROUP)

The need for greater defence against air attack resulted in the size of these ships being considerably larger than their immediate predecessors. Their dimensions were similar to those of the 'Tribal' class but they had greater beam for stability. When under consideration, the Admiralty was still hoping for a twin 4.7in HA mounting but the twin 4.5in was selected, with two turrets being fitted forward.

The sketch design was approved in October 1941 with the building drawings receiving approval in March the following year (they are sometimes referred to as the

'1942 Battle's). Orders for ten ships were placed in April, with another six ships in August.

The close range defence was to be supplied by four 40mm twin Hazemeyer mountings, two side by side amidships and two 'en echelon' aft. This arrangement maximised the firing arcs of these guns. A single 4in mounting, for star shell, was to be carried aft of the funnel but this was only fitted in a few ships: *Armada*, *Barfleur*, *Camperdown* and *Hogue* are usually listed, but there is photographic evidence that *Trafalgar* also carried the gun. The other ships received two single 40mm guns, sited in the same location but with one on each side of the ship. The intention was to complete the close range defence by four single 20mm mountings, two in the bridge wings and two on the quarterdeck, but delays in the availability of the Mk VI DCTs resulted in these being replaced, initially with twin 20mm mountings and eventually with single 40mm mountings.

The delay also resulted in *Cadiz*, *Gravelines*, *St James*, *St Kitts*, *Saintes*, *Sluys*, *Solebay* and *Vigo* receiving twin 40mm STAAG (Stabilised Tachymetric Anti-Aircraft Gun) mountings with radar Type 262 instead of the twin Hazemeyer mountings. *Saintes* was also fitted with the prototype Mk VI twin 4.5in mounting (to be used on the later *Daring* class) in 'B' position.

The armament was completed by two quadruple banks of torpedo tubes, four depth charge throwers and two rails. The DCT was to be fitted with radar Type 275 and the twin 40mm mountings with Type 282. The tripod foremast carried Type 272 and HF/DF, soon replaced with a lattice mast carrying Type 293, and the after pole mast Type 291.

With the increased beam to improve stability came the need for higher engine power to maintain speed but this was achieved with just two boilers. Fin stabilisers were fitted in *Camperdown* and *Finisterre*.

HMS *Barfleur* was the only 'Battle' class destroyer to see operational service in the Second World War and her pennant number for visual signalling purposes was changed to D61 to conform to US Navy requirements whilst she was serving under overall US Navy Command.

Below: The Mk VI director was finally introduced with the 'Ch' group, its large size and prominent radomes for Type 275 being apparent in this September 1945 view of HMS *Chequers*. Although it offered a significant improvement in effectiveness, its great weight required sacrifices to compensate for its weight, including omitting the forward torpedo tubes and fitting only single 20mm in the bridge wings. Newly commissioned, the ship has no pennant number but retains the late-war camouflage scheme.

Left: HMS *Aisne* was one of the first of the '1943 Battles's to complete, although this was not until March 1947. The distinguishing features of the second group were the US Mk 37 director and a fifth 4.5in gun in a single Mk V mounting, added in response to criticism that the previous group lacked astern fire. *(National Museum of the Royal Navy)*

'BATTLE' CLASS (SECOND GROUP)

The second ('1943') group were to use the lighter US Mk 37 DCT fitted with radar Type 275. Consideration was also given to using the Mk VI turret in later ships of the class but the end of the war led to much rethinking and many cancellations and so all were completed with the Mk IV turret.

Six ships were ordered in March 1943 (one of which was cancelled in October 1945, shortly after launch) and fifteen more the following month but only three of these were completed. Three more ships were ordered in June but all three were cancelled in October 1945. Two further ships for the Royal Australian Navy were ordered from Australian shipyards in October 1944; these completed with the new Mk VI mountings.

A single 4.5in mounting was to replace the 4in star shell gun, quintuple torpedo tubes were to replace the quadruple mountings and a Squid A/S mortar was to be fitted aft. Beam was increased but it was still necessary to remove one of the amidships twin 40mm mountings, relocating the remaining one on the centreline, and two of the twin 20mm mountings. The searchlight was also removed and only a single depth charge rail fitted.

The lattice foremast with radar Type 293 was adopted and the after pole mast with Type 291 retained. The remaining amidships 40mm mounting was to be a twin Mk V fitted with radar Type 282 whilst the other STAAG mountings retained Type 262.

Below: A good view of the heavy AA battery carried by the 'Battle' class compared with earlier destroyers, showing off the four Hazemeyer twins aft; the rest of the close range armament comprises a twin 20mm mount in each bridge wing and a single 20mm Oerlikon between the bridge front and 'B' mount. This is the newly completed *Camperdown*, one of the early ships with the 4in star shell gun abaft the funnel. *(By courtesy of David Hobbs)*

■ LEGEND PARTICULARS

'J' & 'K' Classes

Displacement:	1690t (standard), 2330t (full load)
Length:	339ft 6in (pp), 356ft 6in (oa)

Length: 339ft 6in (pp), 356ft 6in (oa)　　Beam:　35ft 9in　　Draught:　12ft 6in (full load)

Machinery: twin shaft, 2 x Parsons single reduction geared turbines, 2 x Admiralty 3-drum boilers

Power/Speed: 40,000shp/36kts (32kts full load)

Armament: 6 x 4.7in/45 QF Mk XII in three twin CPXIX mountings, 4 x 2pdr pom-pom in a quadruple mounting Mk VII, 8 x 0.5in machine guns in two quadruple mountings, 2 x pentad TT for Mk IX or IX* 21in torpedoes

Jervis, F00, *Jackal*, F22, *Jaguar*, F34, *Janus*, F53, *Javelin*, F61, *Jersey*, F72, *Juno*, F46, *Jupiter*, F85 (completed Apr-Sept 1939)

Kelly, F01, *Kandahar*, F28, *Kashmir*, F12, *Kelvin*, F37, *Khartoum*, F45, *Kimberley*, F50, *Kingston*, F64, *Kipling*, F91 (completed Aug 1939-Feb 1940)

'L' Class

Displacement: 1920t (standard), 2660t (full load)

Length: 345ft 6in (pp), 362ft 3in (oa)　　Beam:　37ft　　Draught:　13ft 9in (full load)

Machinery: twin shaft, 2 x Parsons single reduction geared turbines, 2 x Admiralty 3-drum boilers

Power/Speed: 48,000shp/36kts (32.5kts full load)

Armament: 6 x 4.7in/50 QF Mk XI in three twin Mk XX mountings, 4 x 2pdr pom-pom in a quadruple mounting Mk VIII or VIII*, 2 x 20mm in single mounts, 12 x 0.5in machine guns in two quadruple and two twin mountings, 2 x quad Mk X or VIII*** TT for Mk IX** 21in torpedoes

Laforey, F99, *Lance*, F87, *Larne* (re-named *Gurkha* before launch), F63, *Legion*, F74, *Lightning*, F55, *Lively*, F40, *Lookout*, F32, *Loyal*, F15 (completed Dec 1940-Oct 1942)

'M' Class

Displacement: 1920t (standard), 2725t (full load)

Length: 345ft 6in (pp), 362ft 3in (oa)　　Beam:　37ft　　Draught:　14ft (full load)

Machinery: twin shaft, 2 x Parsons single reduction geared turbines, 2 x Admiralty 3-drum boilers

Power/Speed: 48,000shp/36kts (32.5kts full load)

Armament: 6 x 4.7in/50 QF Mk XI in three twin Mk XX mountings, 1 x 4in AA mounting, 4 x 2pdr pom-pom in a quadruple mounting Mk VIII or VIII*, 2 x 20mm in single mounts, 12 x 0.5in machine guns in two quadruple and two twin mountings, 1 x quad Mk X or VIII*** TT for Mk IX** 21in torpedoes

Milne, G14, *Mahratta*, ex-*Marksman*, G23, *Martin*, G44, *Matchless*, G52, *Meteor*, G73, *Musketeer*, G86, *Myrmidon*, G90, *Marne*, G35 (completed Dec 1941-Apr 1943)

'N' Class

Displacement: 1773t (standard), 2384t (full load)

Length: 339ft 6in (pp), 356ft 6in (oa)　　Beam:　35ft 9in　　Draught:　12ft 6in (full load)

Machinery: twin shaft, 2 x Parsons single reduction geared turbines, 2 x Admiralty 3-drum boilers

Power/Speed: 40,000shp/36kts (32kts full load)

Armament: 6 x 4.7in/45 QF Mk XII in three twin CPXIX mountings, 1 x 4in AA mounting, 4 x 2pdr pom-pom in a quadruple mounting Mk VII, 4 x 20mm in single mountings, 4 x 0.5in machine guns in two twin mountings, 1 x pentad TT for Mk IX or IX* 21in torpedoes

Napier, G97, *Nepal*, G25, *Nerissa* (re-named ORP *Piorun* before launch), G65, *Nestor*, G02, *Nizam*, G38, *Noble* (commissioned into service as HNMS *Van Galen*), G84, *Nonpareil* (commissioned into service as HNMS *Tjerk Hiddes*), G16, *Norman*, G49 (completed Dec 1940-May 1942)

'O' Class

Displacement: 1610t (standard), 2270t (full load)

Length: 328ft 9in (pp), 345ft (oa)　　Beam:　35ft　　Draught:　12ft 3in (full load)

Machinery: twin shaft, 2 x Parsons single reduction geared turbines, 2 x Admiralty 3-drum boilers

Power/Speed: 40,000shp/36.75kts (33kts full load)

Armament: 4 x 4.7in/45 QF Mk IX** in four CPXVIII mountings, (4 x 4in Mk V* or V** in four Mk III HA mountings actually fitted to two of the 'O' class and six of the 'P' class vessels, those of the 'O' class later being exchanged for two of the 'P' class to give homogeneity to both flotillas, 4 x 2pdr pom-pom Mk VIII in a quadruple mounting Mk VII, 4 x 20mm in single mountings, 2 x quad Mk VIII TT for Mk IX 21in torpedoes

Onslow, ex-*Pakenham*, G17, *Obdurate*, G39, *Obedient*, G48, *Offa*, G29, *Onslaught*, ex-*Pathfinder*, G04, *Opportune*, G80, *Oribi*, G66, *Orwell*, G98 (completed Jul 1941-Oct 1942)

'P' Class

Displacement: 1640t (standard), 2250t (full load)

Length: 328ft 9in (pp), 345ft (oa)　　Beam:　35ft　　Draught:　12ft 3in (full load)

Machinery: twin shaft, 2 x Parsons single reduction geared turbines, 2 x Admiralty 3-drum boilers

Power/Speed: 40,000shp/36.75kts (33kts full load)

Armament: 5 x 4in Mk V* or V** in five Mk III HA mountings, 4 x 2pdr pom-pom Mk VIII in a quadruple mounting Mk VII, 4 x 20mm in single mountings, 1 x quad Mk VIII TT for Mk IX 21in torpedoes

Pakenham, ex-*Onslow*, G06, *Paladin*, G69, *Panther*, G41, *Partridge*, G30, *Pathfinder*, ex-*Onslaught*, G10, *Penn*, G77, *Petard*, G56, *Porcupine*, G93 (completed Dec 1941-Aug 1942)

'Q' Class

Displacement:	1692t (standard), 2411t (full load)

Length: 339ft 6in (pp), 358ft 3in (oa)   **Beam:** 35ft 9in   **Draught:** 13ft 6in (full load)

Machinery: twin shaft, 2 x Parsons single reduction geared turbines, 2 x Admiralty 3-drum boilers

Power/Speed: 40,000shp/36kts (32kts full load)

Armament: 4 x 4.7in/45 QF Mk IX^{AA} in four CPXVIII mountings, 4 x 2pdr pom-pom M4 in a quadruple mounting Mk VII^A, 6 x 20mm single mountings, 2 x quad mounting TT for Mk IX 21in torpedoes

Quilliam, G09, *Quadrant*, G11, *Quail*, G45, *Quality*, G62, *Queenborough*, G70, *Quentin*, G78, *Quiberon*, G81, *Quickmatch*, G92 (completed Jul 1942-Jan 1943)

'R' Class

Displacement: 1705t (standard), 2425t (full load)

Length: 339ft 6in (pp), 358ft 3in (oa)   **Beam:** 35ft 9in   **Draught:** 13ft 6in (full load)

Machinery: twin shaft, 2 x Parsons single reduction geared turbines, 2 x Admiralty 3-drum boilers

Power/Speed: 40,000shp/36kts (32kts full load)

Armament: 4 x 4.7in/45 QF Mk IX** in four CPXVIII mountings, 4 x 2pdr pom-pom M4 in a quadruple mounting Mk VII*, 6 x 20mm single mountings, 2 x quad mounting TT for Mk IX 21in torpedoes

Rotherham, H09, *Racehorse*, H11, *Raider*, H15, *Rapid*, H32, *Redoubt*, H41, *Relentless*, H85, *Rocket*, H92, *Roebuck*, H95 (completed Aug 1942-Aug 1943)

'S' Class

Displacement: 1710t (standard), 2530t (full load)

Length: 339ft 6in (pp), 362ft 9in (oa)   **Beam:** 35ft 9in   **Draught:** 14ft 6in (full load)

Machinery: twin shaft, 2 x Parsons single reduction geared turbines, 2 x Admiralty 3-drum boilers

Power/Speed: 40,000shp/36kts (32kts full load)

Armament: 4 x 4.7in/45 QF Mk IX or Mk XII in four Mk XXII mountings, 2 x 40mm Bofors in a twin Hazemeyer Mk IV mounting, 8 x 20mm in twin mountings, 2 x quad mounting TT for Mk IX 21in torpedoes

Saumarez, G12, *Scourge*, G01, *Shark* (commissioned into service as HNorMS *Svenner*), G03, *Scorpion*, G07, *Savage*, G20, *Success* (commissioned into service as HNorMS *Stord*), G26, *Swift*, G46, *Serapis*, G94 (completed May 1943-Mar 1944)

'T' Class

Displacement: 1802t (standard), 2530t (full load)

Length: 339ft 6in (pp), 362ft 9in (oa)   **Beam:** 35ft 9in   **Draught:** 14ft 6in (full load)

Machinery: twin shaft, 2 x Parsons single reduction geared turbines, 2 x Admiralty 3-drum boilers

Power/Speed: 40,000shp/36kts (32kts full load)

Armament: 4 x 4.7in/45 QF Mk IX or Mk XII in four Mk XXII mountings, 2 x 40mm Bofors in a twin Hazemeyer Mk IV mounting, 8 x 20mm in twin mountings, 2 x quad mounting TT for Mk IX 21in torpedoes

Troubridge, R00, *Tumult*, R11, *Teazer*, R23, *Terpsichore*, R33, *Tenacious*, R45, *Tuscan*, R56, *Tyrian*, R67, *Termagant*, R89 (completed Mar 1943-Jan 1944)

'U' Class

Displacement: 1777t (standard), 2508t (full load)

Length: 339ft 6in (pp), 362ft 9in (oa)   **Beam:** 35ft 9in   **Draught:** 14ft (full load)

Machinery: twin shaft, 2 x Parsons single reduction geared turbines, 2 x Admiralty 3-drum boilers

Power/Speed: 40,000shp/36kts (32kts full load)

Armament: 4 x 4.7in/45 QF Mk IX or Mk XII in four Mk XXII mountings, 2 x 40mm Bofors in a twin Hazemeyer Mk IV mounting, 8 x 20mm in twin mountings, 2 x quad mounting TT for Mk IX 21in torpedoes

Grenville, R97, *Urania*, R05, *Ursa*, R22, *Undine*, R42, *Undaunted*, R53, *Ulysses*, R69, *Ulster*, R83, *Urchin*, R99 (completed May 1943-Mar 1944)

'V' Class

Displacement: 1808t (standard), 2530t (full load)

Length: 339ft 6in (pp), 362ft 9in (oa)   **Beam:** 35ft 9in   **Draught:** 14ft 6in (full load)

Machinery: twin shaft, 2 x Parsons single reduction geared turbines, 2 x Admiralty 3-drum boilers

Power/Speed: 40,000shp/36kts (32kts full load)

Armament: 4 x 4.7in/45 QF Mk IX or Mk XII in four Mk XXII mountings, 2 x 40mm Bofors in a twin Hazemeyer Mk IV mounting, 8 x 20mm in twin mountings, 2 x quad mounting TT for Mk IX 21in torpedoes

Hardy, R08, *Valentine* (commissioned into service as HMCS *Algonquin*), R17, *Verulam*, R28, *Volage*, R41, *Venus*, R50, *Vixen* (commissioned into service as HMCS *Sioux*), R64, *Virago*, R75, *Vigilant*, R93 (completed Aug 1943-May 1944)

Continued overleaf

'W' Class

Displacement:	1710t (standard), 2530t (full load)			
Length:	339ft 6in (pp), 362ft 9in (oa)	Beam: 35ft 9in	Draught:	14ft 6in (full load)
Machinery:	twin shaft, 2 x Parsons single reduction geared turbines, 2 x Admiralty 3-drum boilers			
Power/Speed:	40,000shp/36kts (32kts full load)			
Armament:	4 x 4.7in/45 QF Mk IX or Mk XII in four Mk XXII mountings, 2 x 40mm Bofors in a twin Hazemeyer Mk IV mounting, 8 X 20mm in twin mountings, 2 x quad mounting TT for Mk IX 21in torpedoes			

Kempenfelt, R03, *Whelp*, R37, *Wrangler*, R48, *Wakeful*, R59, *Wizard*, R72, *Wessex*, R78, *Whirlwind*, R87, *Wager*, R98 (completed Oct 1943-Jul 1944)

'Z' Class

Displacement:	1830t (standard), 2530t (full load)			
Length:	339ft 6in (pp), 362ft 9in (oa)	Beam: 35ft 9in	Draught:	14ft (full load)
Machinery:	twin shaft, 2 x Parsons single reduction geared turbines, 2 x Admiralty 3-drum boilers			
Power/Speed:	40,000shp/36kts (32kts full load)			
Armament:	4 x 4.5in/45 QF Mk IV in four CPV mountings, 2 x 40mm Bofors in a twin Hazemeyer Mk IV mounting, 6 x 20mm in two twin and two single mountings, 2 x quad mounting TT for Mk IX** 21in torpedoes			

Myngs, R06, *Zest*, R02, *Zephyr*, R19, *Zealous*, R39, *Zodiac*, R54, *Zambesi*, R66, *Zebra*, R81, *Zenith*, R95 (completed Jun-Dec 1944)

'Ca' Class

Displacement:	1710t (standard), 2530t (full load)			
Length:	339ft 6in (pp), 362ft 9in (oa)	Beam: 35ft 9in	Draught:	14ft 9in (full load)
Machinery:	twin shaft, 2 x Parsons single reduction geared turbines, 2 x Admiralty 3-drum boilers			
Power/Speed:	40,000shp/36kts (32kts full load)			
Armament:	4 x 4.5in/45 QF Mk IV in four CPV mountings, 2 x 40mm Bofors in a twin Hazemeyer Mk IV mounting, 6 x 20mm in two twin and two single mountings, 2 x quad mounting TT for Mk IX** 21in torpedoes			

Caprice, R01, *Caesar*, R07, *Cavendish*, R15, *Carysfort*, R25, *Carron*, R30, *Cassandra*, R62, *Cavalier*, R73, *Cambrian*, R85 (completed Apr 1944-Feb 1945)

'Ch' Class

Displacement:	1885t (standard), 2545t (full load)			
Length:	339ft 6in (pp), 362ft 9in (oa)	Beam: 35ft 9in	Draught:	15ft 3in (full load)
Machinery:	twin shaft, 2 x Parsons single reduction geared turbines, 2 x Admiralty 3-drum boilers			
Power/Speed:	40,000shp/36kts (32kts full load)			
Armament:	4 x 4.5in/45 QF Mk IV in four CPV mountings, 2 x 40mm Bofors in a twin Hazemeyer Mk IV mounting, 1 x quad QR Mk VIII mounting TT for Mk IX** 21in torpedoes			

Charity, R29,*Chieftain*, R36, *Chevron*, R51, *Chaplet*, R52, *Chivalrous*, R21, *Chequers*, R61, *Cheviot*, R90, *Childers*, R91 (completed Aug 1945-May 1946)

'Co' & 'Cr' Classes

Displacement:	1865t (standard), 2515t (full load)			
Length:	339ft 6in (pp), 362ft 9in (oa)	Beam: 35ft 9in	Draught:	15ft 3in (full load)
Machinery:	twin shaft, 2 x Parsons single reduction geared turbines, 2 x Admiralty 3-drum boilers			
Power/Speed:	40,000shp/36kts (32kts full load)			
Armament:	4 x 4.5in/45 QF Mk IV in four CPV mountings, 4 x 40mm Bofors in a twin and two single mountings, 2 x 20mm in single mountings, 1 x quad QR Mk VIII mounting TT for Mk IX** 21in torpedoes			

Contest, R12, *Comet*, R26, *Cockade*, R34, *Comus*, R43, *Cossack*, R57, *Concord*, R63, *Constance*, R71, *Consort*, R76 (completed Jun 1945-Dec 1946)
Crescent, R16, *Crusader*, R20, *Croziers*, R27, *Cromwell*, R35, *Crystal*, R38, *Crown*, R46, *Crispin*, R68, *Creole*, R82 (completed Sep 1945-Apr 1947)

Battle Class (1st, 1942, group)

Displacement:	2315t (standard), 3290t (full load)			
Length:	355ft (pp), 379ft (oa)	Beam: 40ft 3in	Draught:	15ft 3in (full load)
Machinery:	twin shaft, 2 x Parsons single reduction geared turbines, 2 x Admiralty 3-drum boilers			
Power/Speed:	50,000shp/35.75kts (31.25kts full load)			
Armament:	4 x 4.5in/45 QF Mk III in two Mk IV mountings, 8 x 40mm Bofors in four twin Mk IV mountings, 4 x 20mm in single mountings, 2 x pentad mounting TT for Mk IX 21in torpedoes			

Cadiz, R09, *Armada*, R14, *St Kitts*, R18, *Gravelines*, R24, *Vigo*, R31, *Camperdown*, R32, *Lagos*, R44, *Gabbard*, R47, *Finisterre*, R55, *Sluys*, R60, *St James*, R65, *Solebay*, R70, *Hogue*, R74, *Trafalgar*, R77, *Barfleur*, R80, *Saintes*, R84 (completed Sep 1944-Dec 1946)

Battle Class (2nd, 1943, group)

Displacement:	2380t (standard), 3400t (full load)			
Length:	355ft (pp), 379ft (oa)	Beam: 40ft 6in	Draught:	15ft 3in (full load)
Machinery:	twin shaft, 2 x Parsons single reduction geared turbines, 2 x Admiralty 3-drum boilers			
Power/Speed:	50,000shp/35.75kts (31.25kts full load)			
Armament:	4 x 4.5in/45 QF Mk III in two Mk IV mountings, 1 x 4.5in/45 QF Mk IV in a single Mk V mounting, 8 x 40mm Bofors in three twin and two single mountings, 2 x pentad Mk III TT for Mk IX** 21in. torpedoes			

Agincourt, L06, *Dunkirk*, L09, *Alamein*, L17, *Aisne*, L22, *Matapan*, L43, *Jutland*, L62, *Barrosa*, L68, *Corunna*, L97 (completed Nov 1946-May 1948)

Model Products

The two smallest scales, 1:3000 and 1:2400, are primarily intended for wargamers, allowing the players to re-enact naval battles at realistic 'scale' ranges without requiring enormous playing areas.

DAVCO (SKYTREX)   1:3000 Scale

■ The Davco (Skytrex) models from the UK at 1:3000 scale are very robust and hence ideal for wargaming, the models being just a single piece white metal casting. The models are quite crude, unpainted, do not have masts and are supplied in packs of two identical castings. The level of detail is such as to enable the class of ship to be recognised, although with similar classes this is not always easy. The 'Emergency' designs are available as just two different castings. The castings appear to have too much depth, although at this small scale, this is not really surprising. There are no instructions, just a small sheet of paper containing basic technical details of the vessels. It might be a good idea to paint each vessel (or at least each class) in a

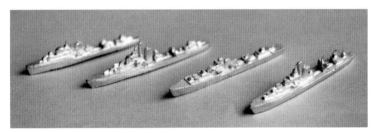

Below: The three DAVCO models of 'J', 'K', 'L', 'M' & 'N' class destroyers.

distinctive manner to assist recognition during a wargame.

Above: The DAVCO models of (from left to right) 'O' & 'P'; 'S', 'T', 'U', 'V' & 'W'; 'C'; and 'Battle' class destroyers.

GHQ   1:2400 Scale

■ The American GHQ models at 1:2400 scale come in bubble packages on brightly coloured card. The plastic bubble packaging is quite stiff but was not sufficient to protect my samples. Two of the castings were badly bent, the funnel and mast, not surprisingly, suffering most. The third casting had a badly warped hull but after cleaning up, a surprisingly detailed model appeared, the tripod mast being particularly impressive for such a small scale. The model comprises just a single, unpainted, one-piece casting. The instructions comprise a simple profile drawing plus limited technical and historical details.

There are no painting details included by either of these manufacturers but many wargamers will be satisfied with an overall grey paint scheme with a limited number of colour highlights, such as black funnel tops.

Above: The single GHQ example of a 'J' class destroyer. Note the tripod mast and the rows of scuttles along the sides of the (unfortunately warped) hull.

EAGLEWALL   1:1200 Scale

■ This long discontinued but well known series of plastic models from a UK company featured just one model of the wartime fleet destroyers in the 'Battle of Narvik Series' – HMS *Kimberley*. There is some attractive artwork on the lid of the box which contains the components to produce either a full hull or waterline model, the above water section being in two parts with the below water section in just a single moulding. The components for the super-structure, funnel, weapons etc are well

Left: The attractive artwork of HMS *Kimberley* on the box top of the kit produced by Eaglewall Plastics Ltd.

moulded and the tripod mast is very fine

considering the moulding techniques in use at the time of manufacture. Although no longer in production, these kits do appear from time to time on eBay.

The instruction sheet includes an assembly diagram, some basic painting details and a short history of the two battles of Narvik.

SUPERIOR MODELS
1:1200 Scale

This American company produce three white metal models of fleet destroyers, each one being a single piece, unpainted waterline casting. These are accurate but detail is limited. Lattice masts are cast as solid with an impression of the lattice work on the surface and so careful painting (no painting details are included) is required to produce a realistic appearance. The lines of scuttles (portholes) are just visible on the hulls and these will need increasing in depth when cleaning up the moulding before painting.

Above: The Superior Models castings of a 'J' class destroyer (left) and the later 'S' class destroyer (right), both representing the ships as in 1944 when fitted with lattice masts.

Right: The Mountford waterline model of HMS *Napier*.

Below: The 'O' and 'P' emergency classes are portrayed in these two models by Navis-Neptun.

MOUNTFORD MINIATURES
1:1250 Scale

Mountford of the UK produce resin castings which are available either

unpainted (as a kit) or painted, as a completed model. The kits are very simple, as is the painting of the complete models (light grey hull and upperworks, dark grey main deck and black gun barrels, mast and funnel top). The hulls are much thinner than those from Superior Models, representing the ships sitting much lower in the water. Being made of resin rather than white metal, they feel very light.

NAVIS-NEPTUN
1:1250 Scale

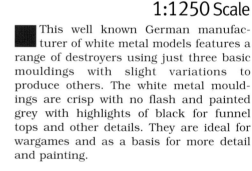

This well known German manufacturer of white metal models features a range of destroyers using just three basic mouldings with slight variations to produce others. The white metal mouldings are crisp with no flash and painted grey with highlights of black for funnel tops and other details. They are ideal for wargames and as a basis for more detail and painting.

Above: The Navis-Neptun models of the earlier 'J', 'K', 'L', 'M' and 'N' classes.

B-RESINA
1:700 Scale

This now discontinued resin kit of HMS *Jupiter* is nicely cast but the details clearly show the great improvements in

casting techniques used today and are best replaced by offerings from other manufacturers.

MATCHBOX

1:700 Scale

■ Another discontinued kit, this time in plastic, also shows the great advances in moulding techniques. The components for HMS *Kelly* were supplied on two different colour sprues. This was a waterline model with the hull provided in two halves with separate deck and waterline sections. There were numerous 'chunky' parts to this kit, the masts in particular being rather thick, but other details, such

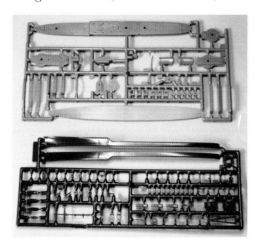

as the gun barrels, were much finer. The instructions only give a simple grey colour scheme, representing the ship as she was before the Second World War and this scheme is reproduced in colour on the back of the box.

An inexpensive model which, with some work and additional details, can produce a good representation of the original ship. Revell should be re-issuing this kit in 2013, the only difference being that both sprues will be moulded in light grey and the instructions will be amended slightly.

Above: The exciting box-top artwork of the Matchbox kit of HMS *Kelly*.

Left: The two differently coloured sprues contain many components.

Below: The top and bottom of the Tamiya box includes an illustration of the ship at sea wearing a camouflage pattern plus some basic painting details of the ship in grey.

TAMIYA

1:700 Scale

■ This kit of the 'O' class destroyers was originally released by Skywave. The box contains two identical models, all the components, apart from the waterline section, being on one sprue. There are far fewer components than in the Matchbox *Kelly* kit, the primary difference being that the hull is a single piece moulding. As the main armament was single barrelled, the barrels are moulded as part of the turret rather than being separate as for the twin barrels in the Matchbox kit.

As with other kits from this Japanese manufacturer, the mouldings are generally fine with thin masts and light AA armament. The fit of components is generally good and alternative mouldings are provided to represent the 4.7in and the 4in gun mountings that were fitted to this class, but there are no optional components to represent the minelaying configuration (but see Accessories). Only one set of torpedo tubes is provided, the aft set being

replaced by a 4in AA gun.

Instructions are provided in the form of assembly diagrams and the decals include

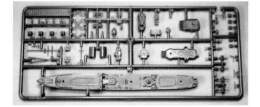

pennant numbers (in both black and white) for eight ships. The sheet also includes two White Ensigns and some depth markings for inclusion on the hull.

Left: One of the two identical sprues provided to construct two vessels.

HP MODELS

1:700 Scale

■ The German company of HP Models offer a wide range of models – three of the 'L' class, one 'M' class, six 'J' class, seven 'K' class and eleven 'Battle' class.

They are all waterline models and there are many shared components, particularly between models of the vessels in the same class.

Right: The components for the 'Battle' class destroyer, HMS *Agincourt*, as supplied by HP Models.

The hull moulding is clean but there is a lot of flash on the smaller components, the majority of which are supplied on thin resin wafers and hence require careful removal. Lattice masts are supplied as solid mouldings with a representation of the lattice framework on the surface. Brass rod is specified for tripod masts, the instructions containing details of thickness and dimensions.

Instructions comprise a large drawing of the ship, an assembly diagram plus diagrams of the contents of the model's rather flimsy box. Although the boxes are thin, the mouldings are well protected by 'bubble wrap' and so any damage is minimal. There are no painting instructions in all of the kits (some do include camouflage patterns) and no etched brass details but the kit does contain a sheet of flags – White and Blue Ensigns at different sizes, Union Jacks, again at different sizes, and Admiral's flags.

Right: Just three of the model kits available from HP Models.

Below: The hull and details, on resin wafers, of HMS *Caesar*.

MOLE MARITIME MODELS   1:700 Scale

This model of the later 'C' class destroyers is considered as a 'semi-kit' from a 'cottage industry' (mastered by Rob Kernaghan) and is available through Dorking Models of the UK. The mouldings are accurate but do require some cleaning up. Instructions are contained on just a single (double sided) A4 sheet and include a drawing plus photographs of the completed model which identify the location of parts. This model does require some additional parts, *eg* torpedo tubes, liferafts etc (which are readily available as they are common to many ships), and a sheet of etched brass is recommended.

This is a different approach to modelling which provides the basic parts for the modeller whilst keeping the cost down. A little more work is required than is required with some other resin kits today, but modellers can produce a truly representative and accurate model.

Above: The 'cottage industry' model of HMS *Caesar* comes in a robust cardboard box and is well packaged.

NIKO MODELS   1:700 Scale

This Polish company produce a single model of *Nizam* (a destroyer that was transferred to Poland), and like other resin kits at this scale, it is a waterline model. The hull and major components require a minimal amount of attention but the smaller components do need to be removed from a sprue and cleaned up a bit. The moulding is fine so care is required here. There is a sheet of etched brass (but no guardrails) and brass rod is used for the tripod and pole masts, dimensions being given on the instruction sheet.

There are no decals and the instruc-

Left: The Niko model is supplied in a solid box with an illustration of the completed model on the lid.

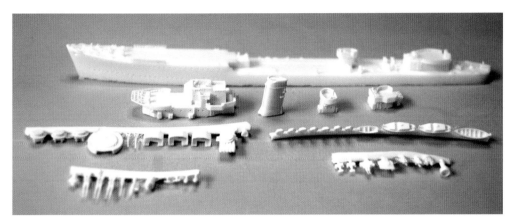

Left: The well cast hull with the major components and minor ones on various sprues. Note the hollow interiors to the shields for the primary armament.

tions comprise just two A4 sheets. These include two assembly diagrams which clearly indicate the location of the many smaller (well cast) components. There is also a drawing of the ship plus some painting instructions.

WHITE ENSIGN MODELS

1:700 Scale

The kits from White Ensign Models (WEM) of the UK are similar in format – a well cast hull (although some are susceptible to warping), parts for the superstructure and some minor components cast on sprues, a sheet of etched brass, plus lengths of brass rod. If constructing the model representing a vessel early in her career then a tripod mast is probably applicable and this can be constructed using either the brass rod or lengths of resin rod, both of which are supplied in the kit. If the model is to represent a vessel later in her career then a lattice mast is more likely and this is supplied on the etched brass sheet.

The instructions, although generally well written and extensive, are not always clear as to which should be fitted and so a little research will be necessary to identify the precise configuration of a particular vessel

Above: The box from WEM includes a colour drawing on the box-top which is a duplicate of one in the instructions.

Left: The many parts in a typical WEM kit (in this case, that for HMS *Milne*) are well cast and include some fine resin rod (bottom right).

at a particular time. For example, the instructions for the 'M' class destroyer, HMS *Milne*, include assembly details for the tripod mast but the drawings and colour details show her as in mid-1943 or December 1944 when a lattice mast had been fitted.

Alternative parts are supplied for some components, *eg* the 4-barrelled pom-pom,

where the item can be assembled from either resin or etched brass, the former generally being 'chunkier' but with more of a 3D appearance while the latter is probably finer but can have a rather flat appearance.

WEM produce six kits of different classes, two of them being for the 'K' class, including the famous *Kelly*.

Below: The box for the Skycraft model of a 'Battle' class destroyer does contain a small picture of the destroyers on the lid.

SKYCRAFT SHIP MODEL   1:600 Scale

These models, now long out of production, were produced by East Anglian Model Supplies of Ipswich in the UK. The kit contains a plan, a two-page instruction leaflet, sandpaper, bits of wood and a small packet with wire and pins. Made in the late 1940s/early 1950s, could this have been the inspiration for the Airfix kits?

SKYTREX   1:600 Scale

Skytrex produce a range of models of smaller craft (the Triton series) which are intended primarily for wargaming and hence are robust in their construction, without a lot of detail. The main hull casting includes the smaller superstructure parts and the boats, but the funnel, bridge, masts and items of armament are cast separately. These mouldings are quite clean and only require a little attention; the main work will be in hollowing out the area under

the boats and their davits. An alternative would be to remove the boats completely and replace them with resin components.

Assembly and painting instructions are non-existent but component locations are clear and so comparison with a suitable photograph or a look at a completed model on the Skytrex website should suffice. These provide a low-cost basis for the modeller who specialises in models at this scale.

Right: The Skytrex white metal model with the major components laid in place.

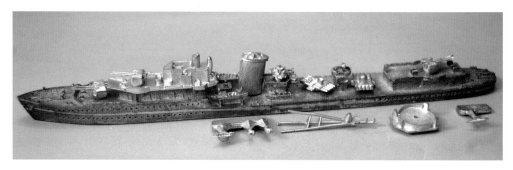

WHITE ENSIGN MODELS   1:350 Scale

The five ships available from WEM ('J', 'K', 'L', 'M' and 'N' classes) are similar in format and include a nicely cast hull, split at the waterline to assist the modeller to produce either a full hull or waterline model. These two sections align well and only a little filler is required for the full hull version. The lower forward part of the

superstructure is moulded integrally with the hull.

Other parts of the superstructure, bridge, funnel, torpedo tubes, primary gun mountings, boats and rangefinder are provided as separate resin castings with the smaller details (*eg* carley floats, secondary armament, etc) being supplied in white

Right: The resin parts for HMS *Janus*.

metal. An extensive etched brass sheet includes item such as guardrails, davits and a lattice mast, while brass rod is provided if the ship is to be modelled whilst having a tripod mast.

The instructions are well thought out and easy to follow with painting instructions given using both WEM's own Colourcoat nomenclature and Admiralty specifications. These kits are highly recommended.

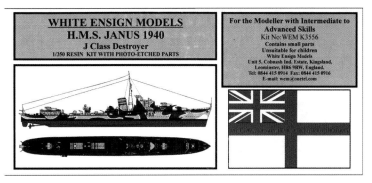

Above: The box for WEM's model of HMS *Janus* carries a small colour diagram which matches the painting details given in the instructions.

COMMANDERS SERIES MODELS 1:350 Scale

Commanders Series Models (Iron Shipwrights) of the USA include two 1:350 scale full hull, resin models of British fleet destroyers in their range – *Lance* and *Onslow*. The hulls are very clean and nicely cast but the kits are rather let down by the smaller components, many of which are not completely formed (particularly the thin bulkheads around parts of the superstructure) and with a lot of flash. A sheet of etched brass is included in each kit and these include guardrails, ladders, platform supports, davits and other details.

The instructions are rather weak. The first page includes a black and white photograph of the actual ship and is followed by one or two pages of illustrations but precise location of some of the

parts is lacking. Painting instructions are also limited, colours being defined by manufacturers' names rather than Admiralty colours.

Above: The nicely moulded hull for the Commander Series Model of HMS *Lance* is rather let down by the quality of the moulding of the smaller parts.

FROG MODELS 1:325 Scale

HMS *Trafalgar* was the very first plastic kit of a British warship and was produced in 1958 by FROG (Flies Right Off the Ground) Models. This is a full hull model with the hull moulded in two halves, and a separate deck. The funnel is also moulded in two halves with the gun barrels moulded separately from the turrets. The lattice mast has four sides but with only one vertical moulded on each part. The mouldings for the superstructure are bare but appear accurate. There is a substantial base for the completed model. There are relatively few components for such a large model.

Instructions are given in twelve assembly diagrams but there are no painting details. A paper sheet of flags is

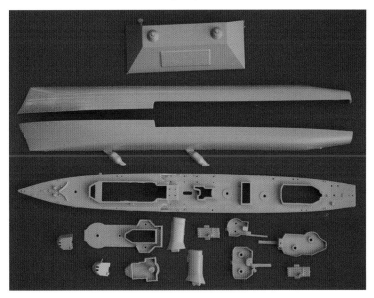

included, as are decals for the pennant numbers on the sides and the stern. This model has been out of production for some years but it does provide a good basis for an accurate, detailed model, further details being either scratchbuilt or made from etched brass.

Above: The larger parts of the FROG kit for HMS *Trafalgar* are well moulded, although rather bare of detail.

Left: The box-top of the FROG model of HMS *Trafalgar* includes some good artwork.

WAK AND MODELIK 1:200 Scale

Each of these three card models are supplied in an A4 size book. Although produced by different manufacturers, they are identical in format and construction. The model is a full hull one. The internal sections

(fore and aft, athwartships and waterline) are printed on thin card which must be affixed to thicker card before construction.

The other parts are printed on thicker card, ready for construction, and coloured

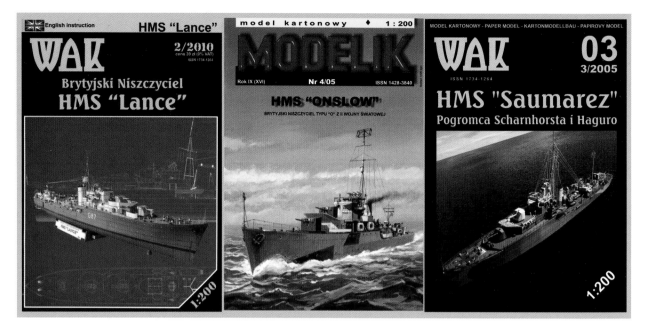

English instruction HMS "Lance"

WAK 2/2010
cena 30 zł (0% VAT)
ISSN 1734-1264

Brytyjski Niszczyciel
HMS "Lance"

model kartonowy ◆ 1 : 200

MODELIK
Rok IX (XVI)   Nr 4/05   ISSN 1428-3840

HMS "ONSLOW"
BRYTYJSKI NISZCZYCIEL TYPU "O" Z II WOJNY ŚWIATOWEJ

MODEL KARTONOWY - PAPER MODEL - KARTONMODELLBAU - PAPIROVY MODEL

WAK 03
3/2005
ISSN 1734-1264

HMS "Saumarez"
Pogromca Scharnhorsta i Haguro

Above: There are Polish card models in 1:200 scale of *Lance*, *Onslow* and *Saumarez*. The covers of the two models from WAK each contain a photograph of a completed model whilst that from Modelik has an artist's impression.

to suit. They are clearly marked as to where to cut and where to bend and contain a high level of detail. These kits include a support to display the completed model and a diagram of the ship identifying the location of parts. Details are supplied for the masts which are best made from brass rod.

Ship and model construction details are provided in Polish, these being duplicated in English for the WAK model of HMS *Lance*.

DEANS MARINE   1:96 Scale

Deans Marine of the United Kingdom offer five different kits (*Grenville*, *Javelin*, *Kelly*, *Solebay* and *Verulam*), all intended for radio-control. These kits include sheets of plasticard for decks and superstructure, a range of resin and white metal fittings and some etched brass in addition to the grp (glass reinforced plastic) hull. Instructions are clear and easy to follow, resulting in a detailed model ideal for sailing. Motors, propellers and shafts are available separately so the modeller can make his own choice but suggestions are included in the instructions.

These are complete kits with the modeller only needing to supply the R/C equipment.

Right: The extensive contents of the Deans Marine kit for HMS *Verulam* is obvious from this photograph.

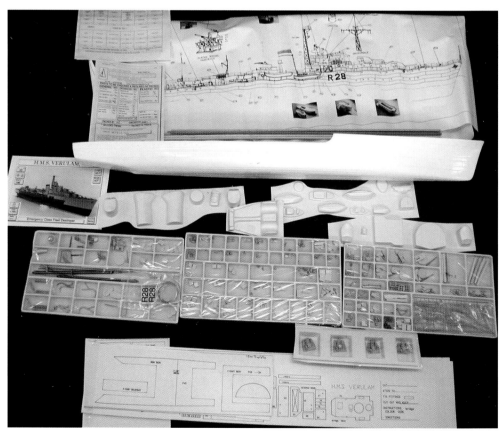

MODELS BY DESIGN

1:96 Scale

■ Models by Design produce just a single grp hull, that for the 'Battle' class destroyer HMS *Cadiz*. The hull is designed for twin screw propulsion and features all plating detail. The plans included are supplied full size and come from the board of the world famous modeller Norman A Ough.

FLEETSCALE (WESTWARD MOULDINGS LTD)

1:96 Scale

■ Two destroyer hulls by John R Haynes are now distributed by Fleetscale. These are an 'O' class (listed as *Onslow*) and a late-war 'S' class.

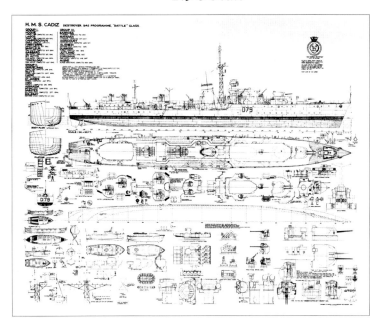

Above: The plan of HMS *Cadiz* from Norman A Ough.

APS MODELS

1:72 Scale

■ The Australian company APS Models produces five different kits of fleet destroyers (*Anzac*, *Quiberon* (both Australian), 'J' class, *Lookout* and *Cavalier* and *Agincourt*) all at this very popular scale for R/C models. Each kit contains a plan and grp hull with a selection of fittings, typically funnel, armament, boats and deck fittings. The hulls are light grey in colour and include plating details. The detailed accessories are cast in resin and some need assembly before being fitted to the hull.

Above. The components and finished assembly of a twin 4.7in gun mounting from APS Models.

Left: A completed model from APS Models: HMS *Quickmatch*, from the *Quiberon* kit.

FLEETSCALE (WESTWARD MOULDINGS LTD **1:72** Scale

■ A hull for HMS *Cavalier* is also available from Fleetscale in the United Kingdom. The hull is similar to that from APS Models and the modeller can also purchase a similar set of fittings. Two sets are available, one for the ship as in 1944 and the other for her when modified later

Left: The resin model of a 40mm gun just needs some rails around the loader's position to complete.

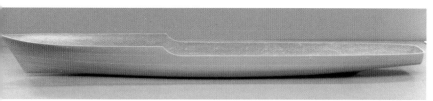

(1960s). Plans and a 'running set' are also available, as are a set of boats, which are manufactured by Quaycraft.

Above: The hull of HMS *Cavalier* from Fleetscale.

Right: The label on the top of the Heritage kit includes a photograph of a completed model which has had much detail added.

Below: The pre-shaped balsa wood supplied for the forward part of the hull and the transom.

HERITAGE KITS

This 'J' class model is an unusual kit, aimed at the modeller who wants to 'scratchbuild' a model whilst minimising cost and limiting the amount of work required. The kit comprises balsa and plywood components, together with a brass rudder. The balsa has been pre-shaped for parts such as the hull, gun mountings and funnel, but all these parts require a considerable amount of shaping and sanding to complete. The hull is slightly simplified in shape, the sides being straight and parallel. The plywood for the decks has been laser

1:72 Scale

cut to shape and also includes watertight doors, hatches etc.

This kit provides a helpful, low cost approach for the newcomer to the hobby who does not want the expense of a grp hull.

Accessories

Right: Part of the sheet of etched brass from Gold Medal Models for 'World War Two British Warships'. The majority of this fret contains parts for larger ships but it also includes the funnel grille, yardarms, depth charge rails and railings for the 'O' class.

Standard etched brass accessories, such as guardrails, ladders, watertight doors etc, at the commonly used scales for smaller models (particularly 1:700 and 1:350), are available from a number of suppliers including White Ensign Models of the United Kingdom, L'Arsenal of France, Eduard of the Czech Republic and Gold Medal Models and Tom's Modelworks of the USA. One item which frequently enhances a model and gives a sense of scale are figures. Again many of these manufacturers can supply etched brass figures at both 1:700 and 1:350 scale but if the modellers wants his figures to have more of a 3D appearance, resin figures at 1:350 scale are available from L'Arsenal and plastic ones from Tamiya of Japan.

'Standard' accessories, such as boats, again at common scales, are also available from a number of sources and these permit modellers to enhance and modify basic kits to produce an endless number of variations of these numerous destroyers. White Ensign Models also market a set of paints (Colourcoats) to match Admiralty definitions.

Although not aimed specifically at the fleet destroyers, Gold Medal Models produce a sheet of etched brass at 1:700 scale for 'World War Two British Warships' (700-5) which contains many parts of use, particularly if modifying a kit to represent a particular vessel at a specific time in its

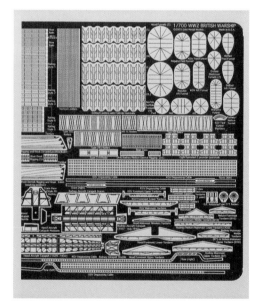

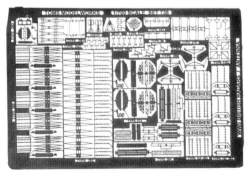

Right: Tom's Modelworks produces a sheet of etched brass for British radars.

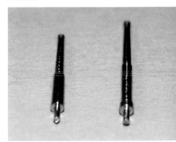

Left: The resin mines available from Admiralty Modelworks.

career. Likewise, Tom's Modelworks produces a sheet (#738) of 'WWII British Radars and Antennas'. If the modeller wants to model one of the destroyers as a minelayer, then the sets of mines from Admiralty Modelworks will also be particularly useful.

Below: The two sheets of etched brass in the Lion Roar set to enhance the Tamiya kit of an 'O' class destroyer.

LION ROAR

The Chinese company of Lion Roar produce an etched brass set for HMS *Onslow* (LE700101) to accompany the Tamiya kit. It consists of two sheets which contain guardrails, the lattice mast, details for the radars and armament, davits and various deck details. The instructions are on three A4 sides and are simple to follow.

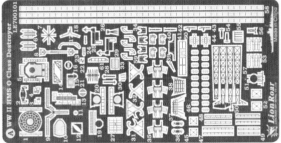
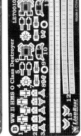

WHITE ENSIGN MODELS

WEM produce a similar set for the Tamiya kit, the contents being very much the same. The set is more generic than that from Lion Roar and includes alternative parts, such as a short lattice mast.

WEM also market etched brass sheets from their own kits of fleet destroyers. The instructions that accompany these show how to use the components but, as the etched brass sheets are to match their own

Left: The 'generic' etched brass sheet from WEM includes alternative parts to suit both 'O' and 'P' class destroyers.

kits, a little research may be required if modelling a different vessel, particularly if at a different date to the basic model.

WEM also market two sets of etched brass at 1:350 scale, again from their own resin kits. These are very extensive sets, including lattice masts, gun and funnel details as well as railings, ladders and davits. Again, some research will be necessary to accurately model a different vessel to that in the basic kit.

Far left: The two etched brass sheet from WEM kits for the 'J', 'K' & 'N' and the 'L' & 'M' class destroyers.

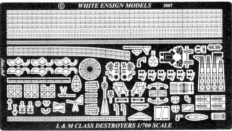

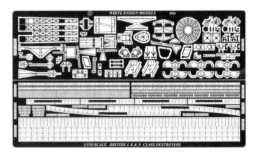

Left: The 1:350 scale etched brass sheet from WEM for the 'J', 'K' & 'N' class destroyers is very extensive, offering many options.

Below: The two different lengths (45- and 50-calibre) of brass barrels from BMK are clearly visible.

BKM & GPM

Also at 1:350 scale, the German firm of Burkhardt Masch Kleinserien (BMK) manufacture a wide range of brass gun barrels, those for 4.7in guns being applicable to the fleet destroyers. Both 45- and 50-calibre barrels are available and are accurately turned and hollow to represent the bore hole at the muzzle.

Turned brass barrels are also available, from GPM of Poland, to enhance the card models from WAK and Modelik. Both primary and secondary barrels are provided

which will be a great improvement (and easier) on the rolled card versions contained as part of the basic kit.

Left: The set of brass barrels (three different calibres) from GPM for the model of HMS *Lance*.

Far right: Twin 20mm Oerlikon power mount kit at 1:96 scale [JRH635].

Right: Quad 2pdr pom-pom mounting at 1:96 scale [JRH378].

Below: John R Haynes 4in Mk IV HA gun in 1:350 scale [JRH782].

JOHN R HAYNES

This well known professional model-maker also has an extensive range of warship fittings in white metal, resin and PE. Most are in the larger scales, but there are a few items at 1:350, including a 4in Mk

IV (JRH782), the single gun that replaced the after torpedo tubes in many wartime destroyers. For those wanting to build larger working models, there are many fittings at 1:96 and even 1:72 scales. Full details can be found at: www.johnrhaynes.com/shop

▦ AVAILABLE MODELS AND KITS

DAVCO (1:3000 scale)

D1510 'J/K/N' class 1938

D1509 *Lance* class 1940

D1508 'L/M' class 1940

D1507 'P' class 1941

D1506 'S-Z' class 1941

D1505 'Battle' 1943

D1504 'C' class 1943

GHQ Models (1:2400 scale)

UKN6 'J' class

Navis Neptun (1:1250 scale)

1160 'L/M' class

1160a 'L/M' class 1943

1160b *Lance* class

1162 'O/P' class 1941

1162a 'O/P' class 1943

1163 'J/K/N' class 1939

1163a 'J/K/N' class 1943

Mountford Miniatures (1:1250 scale)

MM138 'N' class – HMAS *Napier*

MM111 'K' class destroyer

Superior Models (1:1200 scale)

B602 'J' class 1944

B603 'L' & 'M' class 1944

B604 'S-Z' class 1944

Tamiya (1:700 scale) – previously Skywave

TA30194 'O' class destroyer

HP Models (1:700 scale)

GB-040 'L' class *Laforey*

GB-041 'L' class *Lance*

GB-042 'L' class *Legion*

GB-043 'M' class *Martin*

GB-101 'J' class *Jervis*

GB-102 'J' class *Jackal*

GB-103 'J' class *Javelin*

GB-104 'J' class *Juno*

GB-105 'J' class *Jupiter*

GB-106 'J' class *Janus*

GB-107 'K' class *Kelly*

GB-108 'K' class *Kandahar*

GB-109 'K' class *Kashmir*

GB-110 'K' class *Kelvin*

GB-111 'K' class *Kimberley*

GB-112 'K' class *Kingston*

GB-113 'K' class *Kipling*

GB-151 'Battle' class 1942 R80 *Barfleur* Gr1 [with 4in]

GB-152 'Battle' class 1942 R74 *Hogue* Gr1

GB-153 'Battle' class 1942 R32 *Camperdown* Gr1

GB-154 'Battle' class 1942 R77 *Trafalgar* Gr1

GB-155 'Battle' class 1942 R09 *Cadiz* Gr2 [without 4in]

GB-156 'Battle' class 1942 R14 *Armada* Gr2

GB-157 'Battle' class 1942 R70 *Solebay* Gr2

GB-158 'Battle' class 1942 R84 *Saintes* Gr2

GB-159 'Battle' class 1942 R65 *St James* Gr2

GB-160 'Battle' class 1943 I06 *Agincourt* Gr3

GB-161 'Battle' class 1943 I09 *Dunkirk* Gr3

Mole Maritime Models (1:700 scale)

HMS *Caesar*

Niko (1:700 scale)

HMS *Nizam*

White Ensign Models (1:700 scale)

K 715 HMS *Kashmir* 1939, 'K' class destroyer

K 722 HMS *Kelly* 1940, 'K' class destroyer

K 724 HMS *Jervis* 1945, 'J' class destroyer

K 750 'M' class destroyer

K 751 'L' class destroyer

K 754 'V' class destroyer

Skytrex (1:600 scale)

CF44 HMS *Javelin*

CF44A HMS *Kelly*

White Ensign Models (1:350 scale)

K 3519 HMS *Musketeer*, 'M' class destroyer

K 3521 HMS *Laforey*, 'L' class destroyer

K 3556 HMS *Janus* 1940, 'J' class destroyer

K 3557 HMS *Kelly* 1941, 'K' class destroyer

K 3558 'N' class destroyer

Iron Shipwright (1:350 scale)

4-036 HMS *Lance*, 'L' class destroyer (1941)

4-037 HMS *Onslow*, 'O' class destroyer

Modelik (1:200 scale)

Nr4/05 HMS *Onslow*

WAK (1:200 scale)

3/2005 HMS *Saumarez*

2/2010 HMS *Lance*

Deans Marine (1:96 scale)

HMS *Grenville*

HMS *Javelin*

HMS *Kelly*

HMS *Solebay*

HMS *Verulam*

Models by Design (1:96 scale)

HMS *Cadiz*

APS Models (1:72 scale)

HMS *Agincourt*

HMAS *Anzac*

HMAS *Quiberon*

'J', 'K' & 'N' class

HMS *Lookout*

HMS *Cavalier*

Fleetscale (Westward Mouldings Ltd) (1:72 scale)

HMS *Cavalier*

Heritage Kits (1:72 scale)

Javelin class destroyer

Modelmakers' Showcase

TAMIYA *ONSLOW* 1:700 scale

By FILIPE RAMIRES

This model is built from the Tamiya kit with the addition of etched brass rails and many more small details built from scratch.

MOLE MARITIME MODELS **CAVALIER** 1:700 scale By PETER FULGONEY

Peter bought this little kit as Mole Maritime Models late-war destroyer HMS *Caesar* and borrowed some plans which showed all the detail which the instructions unfortunately lack. He also checked the actual *Cavalier* at Chatham. The problem is the later refits, and Peter especially wanted the wartime version, so after some detective work he could see what might be needed but the actual plans were indispensable for the level of detail he required.

Like all fine waterline kits, the box contents are sparse but this is reflected in the price, and there is no heap of parts that are unusable or not wanted. Peter had some spare kit parts, and a couple of destroyer PE frets, which was a start. He did, however, scratch-build the Mk 9 depth charge thrower, and the twin Oerlikon gun. The kit is value for money but not short of pin holes, and the hull was quite bendy and Peter was not able to fully glue it all down – the other way instead of boiling it – to straighten it out.

In all, the model as presented turned out satisfactorily, getting second prize at a local show, but what Peter had always wanted to do was put such a subject into a frozen north scenario – it represents the ship off the Kola Peninsula in 1945 – so he could go to town with the PVA ice, and icy sparkles frozen water effects. All great fun, and he can't wait to do it all again soon.

Material used: rigging – caenis line and stretched sprue combo; paints – Humbrol enamels; glue – pva; PE – White Ensign KG5, and Lion Roar 'O' class; weathering – Mig rust, city dirt, and white ashes – some white ashes also used for snow.

FROG *CORUNNA* 1:325 scale

By PHIL REEDER

A kit first released over fifty years ago but Phil decided to try and build it using modern accessories. It was to be built as HMS *Corunna*, a 1943 'Battle'. After much work the only things left of the original kit were the hull, funnel, 4.5' turrets, torpedo tubes and the ships boats; the rest was scratch-built and photo etch.

WHITE ENSIGN MODELS *JANUS* 1:350 scale

By IAN RUSCOE

This kit from White Ensign Models was essentially built straight out of the box, in its full hull configuration. Like all WEM kits in this scale, extra parts are provided on the photo etch brass sheet to make

others in the same class. The cast resin parts were spotless and the cast white metal examples required only a little cleaning up. When it came to applying the complex camouflage scheme worn by the vessel Ian carefully airbrushed the light grey and blue grey colours and then picked in by hand the white borders where these colours meet as well as the rest of the detail painting. To apply the paint chipping and rust effects he started by carefully hand painting the 'scratches/chips' using a very fine brush and various greys and red browns from the Vallejo range of acrylic paints, using archive photographs as a guide to amount and location. After receiving a coat of matt varnish to protect the paintwork, the model was weathered using various washes of oil base paints to 'lift and emphasise' the detail on the model.

WHITE ENSIGN MODELS *MILNE* 1:700 scale

By PETER FULGONEY

It's a great occasion when White Ensign Models market a new kit, and HMS *Milne* was such an event. Peter is very happy with the level of detail, and the presentation of the kit. The instructions are sufficient and always include a coloured diagram to base the painting scheme on. Another advantage is that the colours are all referenced and available from White Ensign Models themselves in their 'Colorcoats' range which features authentic colour matches. Looking back he believes the only other imports to the kit were the rigging, and crew figures which could be left off if desired.

TAMIYA *OBDURATE* 1:700 scale   By PETER FULGONEY

This is a build from the Tamiya 'O' class destroyer which comes in a two-kit pack. The quality and detail is of its time. However, with the inclusion of Lion Roar photo etch, and a dramatic colour scheme, a reasonable 1:700 scale representation of a Second World War destroyer can be realised. The drawback with this kit for the 'O' class in general is that there are two versions – four were fitted for minelaying and carried 4in guns. HMS *Obdurate* has therefore been altered to allow for this difference. Alterations are always a risk but maybe not so much on a 1970s plastic ship model which can finally be saved with some inspiring detail off the Lion Roar fret.

Whichever model Peter builds, of any class, depends on the name of the ship, and colour scheme and with this qualification in mind, HMS *Obdurate* has both attributes in abundance. The only other requirement Peter needs in his build is composition. With a small destroyer model it can be set off well in a diorama, and the escort carrier, HMS *Biter*, provides this enhancement. Peter has depicted a refuelling exercise called a 'RAS' (Refuelling At Sea), something shown on a Roland Smith DVD featuring the Royal Navy in the Second World War, by the way, and excellent reference for the RN ship modeller today.

WHITE ENSIGN MODELS *ONSLOW* 1:350 scale

By PHIL REEDER

This is a White Ensign Models 1:350 scale kit of the *Kelly*, converted to HMS *Onslow*. Phil used the plans from the *Profile Morskie* book and those from John Lambert. The conversion was more involved than first thought and required nearly all the superstructure to be scratch-built. The 4.7in guns were also scratch-built.

SCRATCH-BUILT *ONSLOW* 1:192 scale By PHILIP REED

Now a well-known professional model-maker, Phil made this *Onslow* model in his earlier days. The hull was carved from a pine block, but most of the rest of the construction was in plastic card, and the level of detail speaks for itself. His methods are covered at length in his book *Waterline Warships* (Seaforth 2010), which describes the building of his model of the destroyer HMS *Caesar*.

SCRATCH-BUILT *VIGO* 1:64 scale By SIR NORMAN PETERS

Despite the impressive level of detail, this model of a 1942 'Battle' was intended to be a working model (although no running gear was actually fitted). Currently in the National Maritime Museum, their records show it to be the work of Sir Norman Peters, built between 1971 and 1982; it is nearly 6ft long. The model shows the later appearance of the class, when the four Hazemeyer mountings were replaced by two STAAGs aft, with an extra deckhouse built on the midships platform. Built from plans by Norman Ough, *Vigo* is depicted as tender to the gunnery training school HMS *Excellent* between 1954 and 1958.

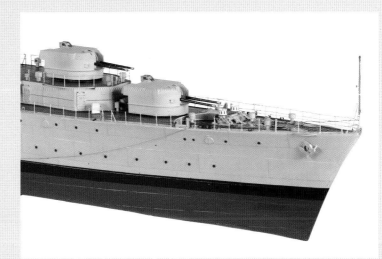

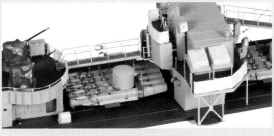

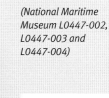

(National Maritime Museum L0447-002, L0447-003 and L0447-004)

WHITE ENSIGN MODELS *KELLY* 1:350 scale By IAN RUSCOE

This is the White Ensign Models resin kit of Mountbatten's famous command HMS *Kelly*. The model was built to show the destroyer at speed with her gun crews at action stations. The kit needs a little extra work to complete *Kelly* as seen, in the form of additional 20mm Oerlikon platforms and some additional 'splinter matting'. Although the latter is provided in the kit's photo etch sheet, Ian found there was not enough and sourced some additional amounts from another WEM 'J, K & N' kit. All went together very easily but then came that colour Mountbatten pink – which is not really pink but more violet in colour. The parts were spray painted in the Mountbatten Pink then 'post shaded' in a lighter tone of the original colour to add some sense of realism. The remaining colours, including any paint chipping on the hull, were carefully picked out by hand using fine tipped paint brushes. Once complete, the model was sprayed in a matt varnish to protect the paintwork before the weathering was carried out. This took the form of oil based paint washes applied to the model. The model was rigged using fine fishing line that was glued into place before

being carefully painted. The figures seen on the model are from L'Arsenal from their cast resin figure sets with pieces of stretched sprue for the shells carried by figures in the gun crews. These were primed and then painted individually before being glued into place on the ship. Finally the completed model was mounted onto its base and the seascape formed and painted around it.

HP MODELS *KINGSTON* 1:700 scale By MIKE McCABE

Mike used the HP Models kit of HMS *Javelin* as the basis for this model and used the WEM etched brass set to add details and the GMM ultrafine railings. Firstly a piece of plasticard was added to the bottom of the hull so that the models could be displayed heeling over. The kit goes together quite well but Mike replaced the main guns and the pom-poms with accessories from Niko. The aircraft is an Italian SM84 torpedo bomber from WEM.

WHITE ENSIGN MODELS *MILNE* 1:700 scale
By IAN RUSCOE

As a change from his usual method of displaying a ship model 'running' at sea Ian thought he would display *Milne* at anchor, supposedly at Malta in January 1945. The White Ensign Models kit is an excellent subject with lots of moulded detail and relatively easy and quick to assemble. The harbour vessel came from a Tamiya Harbour set (although possibly Fujimi are producing it now); the chosen 'lighter' was embellished with photo etch parts including davits, doors and hatches etc from some leftover parts from a WEM cruiser PE set Ian had lying around in the spares box. The buoy is made from one half of a 1:72 scale oil drum and the figures are from Gold Medal Models Naval Figures set.

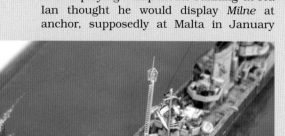

WHITE ENSIGN MODELS ORP *PIORUN* EX-HMS *NERISSA*
1:350 scale
By IAN RUSCOE

With this model Ian wanted to portray *Piorun* in a heavy sea at the time when she was patrolling the English Channel after the D-Day landings when the Channel storms hit the area. The model was built full hull except for the propellers and rudder as these were not going to be seen. After completing the build and painting etc of the model it was mounted onto its base and the procedure of building the choppy sea began, first with a thick mix of interior filler (Polyfilla) which was sculpted as seen, then after drying the crests were added using thin strands of moistened cotton wool that is attached using PVA glue. Once dry

ORP PIORUN
English Channel June 1944

the crests were re-coated in PVA to get rid of any 'furry' appearance. When fully dry any unwanted strands were simply snipped away with a pair of scissors before the painting took place. To simulate the streams of water running off the fore deck and sides of the hull Ian simply sprayed it in place after applying the colour to the seascape.

SCRATCH-BUILT RNethNS *PIET HEIN* EX-*SERAPIS* 1:96 scale

By JOHN R HAYNES

A commission for the Scheepvaart Museum in Amsterdam, the model depicts this 'S' class destroyer after transfer to the Netherlands Navy in 1952, although much of the detail is the same as it was at the end of the war.

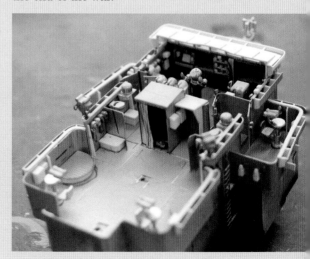

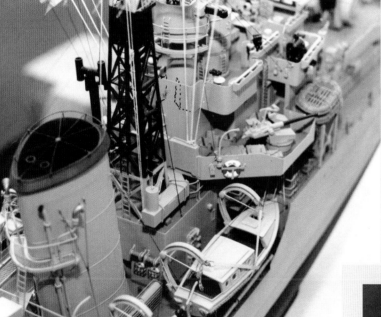

WHITE ENSIGN MODELS *MUSKETEER* 1:350 scale   By IAN RUSCOE

Ian wanted to portray *Musketeer* at sea and so built the WEM kit as a waterline model. The model was built as per instructions with no additional parts except figures and rigging material. The fit of the parts was as to be expected – excellent with no fit issues and although the metal cast parts did require some cleaning, the resin castings were faultless. The kit allows the modeller to build the model as any of the 'M' class ships and even some of the 'L' class with similar fit and layout, although the instructions only direct you on building it as *Musketeer*. The figures used on this occasion are the Fujimi fully rounded plastic figures (two sets are available, static and action poses).

'K' class destroyer – Mountbatten pink, late 1940

■ MOUNTBATTEN PINK - LIGHT (1940)

'M' class destroyer – Western Approaches Pattern, circa 1941 onwards

WHITE ■ B 55 decks ■ B 30

'M' class destroyer – Admiralty Intermediate Disruptive Pattern, 1942-1944

■ G 10 ■ G 45 ■ G 20 decks ■ G 10

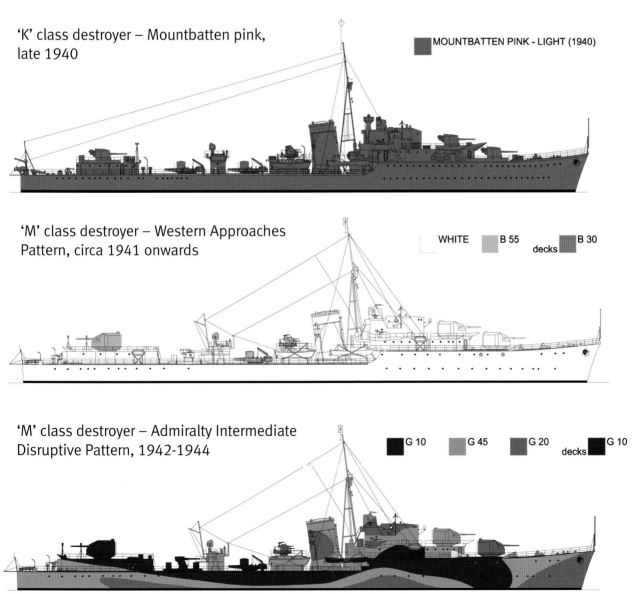

'M' class destroyer – Admiralty Light
Disruptive pattern, 1942-1944

| B 55 | G 45 | B 30 | G 10 | decks | G 20 |

'N' class destroyer – Western Approaches
Pattern, circa 1941 onwards

| WHITE | B 30 | B 55 | decks | B 30 |

'N' class destroyer – Admiralty Intermediate
Disruptive Pattern, 1942-1944

| G 5 | B 15 | B 30 | G 45 | decks | G 10 |

'N' class destroyer – Admiralty Light
Disruptive Pattern, 1942-1944

| B 55 | G 45 | B 30 | G 10 | decks | G 20 |

'O' class destroyer – Western Approaches
Pattern, circa 1941 onwards

| WHITE | B 30 | B 55 | decks | B 30 |

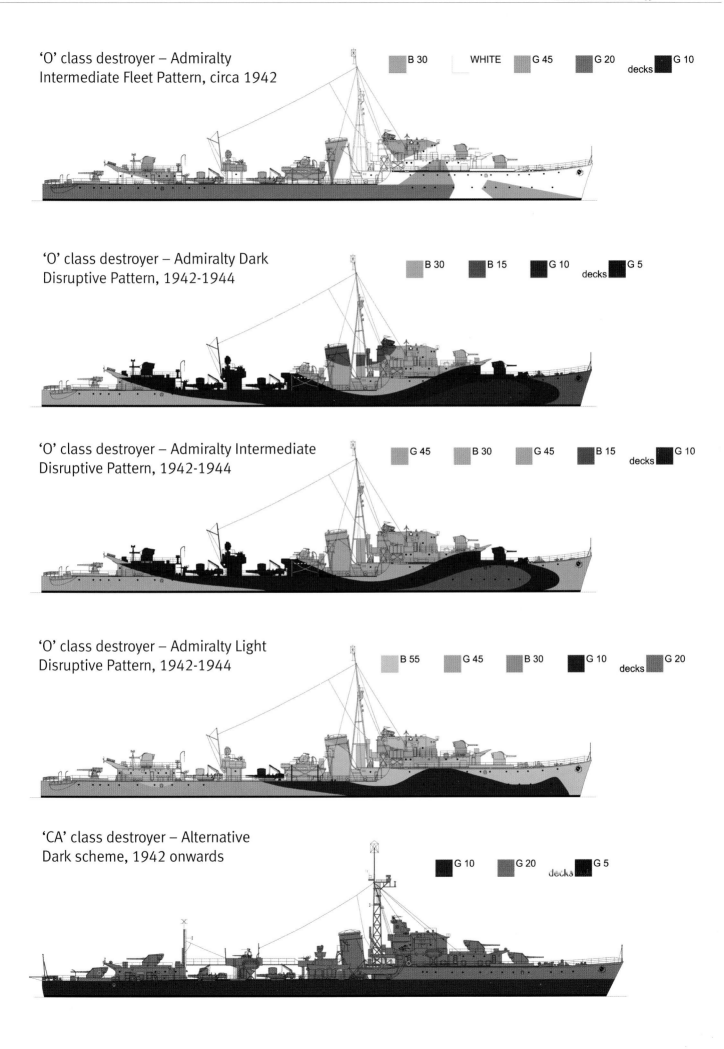

'O' class destroyer – Admiralty Intermediate Fleet Pattern, circa 1942

B 30   WHITE   G 45   G 20   decks G 10

'O' class destroyer – Admiralty Dark Disruptive Pattern, 1942-1944

B 30   B 15   G 10   decks G 5

'O' class destroyer – Admiralty Intermediate Disruptive Pattern, 1942-1944

G 45   B 30   G 45   B 15   decks G 10

'O' class destroyer – Admiralty Light Disruptive Pattern, 1942-1944

B 55   G 45   B 30   G 10   decks G 20

'CA' class destroyer – Alternative Dark scheme, 1942 onwards

G 10   G 20   decks G 5

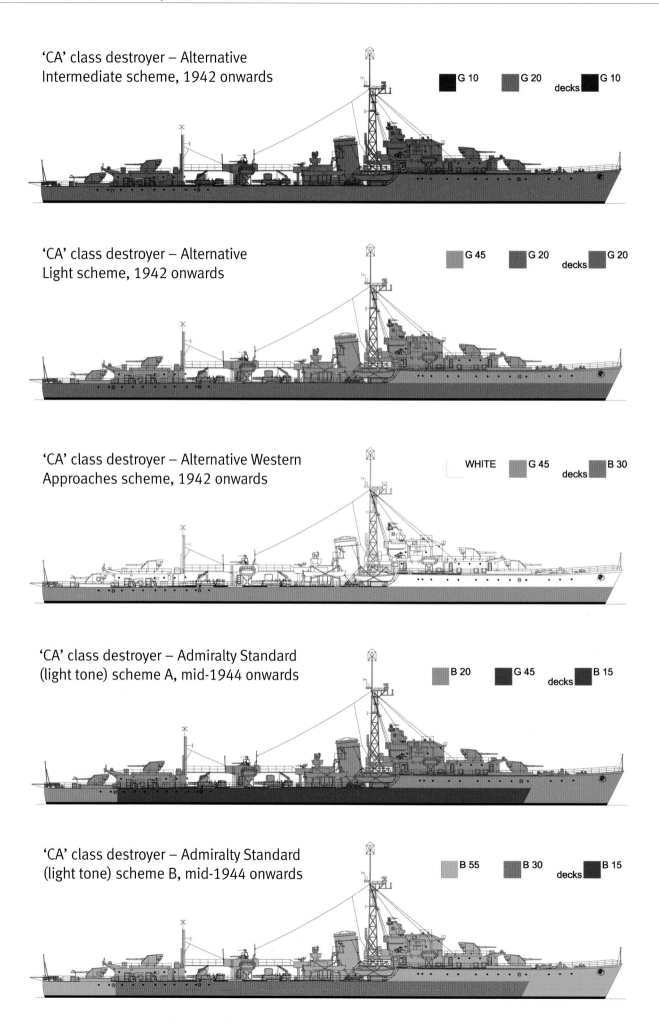

'CA' class destroyer – Alternative
Intermediate scheme, 1942 onwards

G 10   G 20   decks   G 10

'CA' class destroyer – Alternative
Light scheme, 1942 onwards

G 45   G 20   decks   G 20

'CA' class destroyer – Alternative Western
Approaches scheme, 1942 onwards

WHITE   G 45   decks   B 30

'CA' class destroyer – Admiralty Standard
(light tone) scheme A, mid-1944 onwards

B 20   G 45   decks   B 15

'CA' class destroyer – Admiralty Standard
(light tone) scheme B, mid-1944 onwards

B 55   B 30   decks   B 15

Camouflage

A full discussion of this subject requires a book in itself – and one much larger than this publication (see References) and this section should be considered merely as an introductory outline. The only way to be certain of the camouflage worn by a specific ship at a particular time is to obtain photographs with well defined (and confirmed) dates and then, as the majority of photographs are in black and white only (and those that are in colour can be misleading), there is still a query regarding the precise colours used.

The first attempt by the Admiralty to standardise paint schemes came in a Fleet Order issued in 1941, which defined regulations regarding the painting of boot topping. This was followed in 1942 by a more detailed order which gave details of the types of paint to be used. At this time, camouflage patterns were being produced by the Directorate of Camouflage (then based at Leamington Spa) but these were only for larger ships (cruisers, battleships and aircraft carriers) and the patterns to be used on destroyers and below were left to the individual ideas of ships' officers.

It was not until 1943 that a handbook was issued and this included a number of 'standard' designs for smaller ships (from destroyers downwards), but these were only for guidance with individual ships producing their own specific patterns. (For illustrations of these 'standard' patterns, see the Colour Schemes on pages 46-48.)

In general, destroyers carried the same pattern on both port and starboard sides. The Directorate of Camouflage continued to produce individual patterns for the larger ships. The handbook also contained a certain amount of information concerning the theory of camouflage to assist in the design of patterns by the ship's own staff.

The Admiralty produced three 'disruptive' schemes – light, intermediate and dark. Each consisted of a number of irregular areas covering the vertical surfaces and used up to five different tones or colours. The 'light' pattern was intended for use in overcast northern waters with the 'dark' intended for use in areas where the weather was generally finer.

At the beginning of the war, two shades of grey were available in large quantities – AP507A and AP507C – and it was not until 1943 that quantities of other colours

Above: HMS *Kandahar* at Alexandria in mid-1941 carries her revised pennant number, in black, and a distinctive camouflage pattern in AP507C and AP507A (an over-paint of an earlier three-colour scheme traces of which remain). The aft gun is still stowed facing forwards. *(National Museum of the Royal Navy)*

Below: HMS *Nepal* in May 1942, wearing a distinctive Admiralty Disruptive camouflage pattern in MS1 and MS4, with a white pennant number. *(National Maritime Museum N11863)*

Above: HMS *Quality* newly completed in August 1942. The main gun mounts point directly towards the photographer in order to reduce the opportunity for an observer to deduce the calibre. The light AA of six single 20mm Oerlikons are concentrated on the searchlight platform (four) with one in each bridge wing. This dramatic camouflage pattern was confined to this ship and three sisters: *Quickmatch*, *Quilliam* and *Queenborough*. Note how items of equipment (such as the torpedo tubes) are painted in accordance with the adjacent camouflage colour. *(US National Archives via Roger Torgeson)*

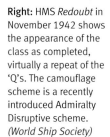

Right: HMS *Redoubt* in November 1942 shows the appearance of the class as completed, virtually a repeat of the 'Q's. The camouflage scheme is a recently introduced Admiralty Disruptive scheme. *(World Ship Society)*

Above: The only 'V' class ship completed with a tripod mast was HMS *Venus*, which carried the Type 291 air warning radar at the topmast head, so the HF/DF aerial normally carried in that position was place atop a short lattice mast fitted to her aft superstructure. As shown here, on completion the ship carried no surface search radar. *(National Museum of the Royal Navy)*

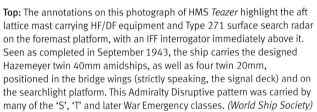

Top: The annotations on this photograph of HMS *Teazer* highlight the aft lattice mast carrying HF/DF equipment and Type 271 surface search radar on the foremast platform, with an IFF interrogator immediately above it. Seen as completed in September 1943, the ship carries the designed Hazemeyer twin 40mm amidships, as well as four twin 20mm, positioned in the bridge wings (strictly speaking, the signal deck) and on the searchlight platform. This Admiralty Disruptive pattern was carried by many of the 'S', 'T' and later War Emergency classes. *(World Ship Society)*

Above: HMS *Zambesi* is painted with a dark grey triangular shape panel on her bow and a medium grey panel at the forecastle break, above the dark grey. The rest of the class had two single 20mm abreast the searchlight, but in this ship they were power-operated twins. *(Naval Photograph Club)*

Top: HMS *Urania* as completed in 1943. The Type 272 'lantern' on mast platform is very evident. (Maritime Photo Library 2099)

Above: *Milne* in December 1944 after a significant refit. The ship now has both banks of torpedo tubes, and the bridge-wing Oerlikons are in twin power-operated mountings. The lattice foremast carries radar Type 276 with a HF/DF aerial on the topmast and the Type 291 antenna relocated to a light pole mast aft. The colour scheme is the standard late-war Admiralty Type A pattern.

Left: For a few months after completion in 1942 HMS *Obdurate* wore this light Western Approaches camouflage scheme of blue and white, also carried by *Onslaught*. (US National Archives via Roger Torgeson)

Above: HMAS *Quiberon* wearing the late-war Admiralty Standard scheme but before the pennant number was changed for service in the Pacific (the very light area on the upper bow is probably not a third colour but simply a newly painted patch of the overall grey). Since completion she has had twin 20mm power mountings added in the bridge wings.

Below: *Charity* in November 1945 demonstrates one variation in the close range armament in this class: the single 2pdrs abaft the funnel instead of 40mm Bofors, with the single 20mm in the bridge wings and the Hazemeyer mounting requiring three separate types of small-calibre ammunition. Note the boat stowed where the forward torpedo tubes should be. *(National Maritime Museum N12034)*

became readily available (at least in Great Britain but not necessarily overseas). The Admiralty defined colours with a letter/number combination starting with the MS series. These varied from MS1 (a very dark grey) to MS4A (a very light grey). A touch of blue could be incorporated, either B5 (Dark Blue-Grey) or B6 (Blue). In the early days of the war, ships mixed their own paint colours but by the time the handbook was issued, a range of pre-mixed paints was available.

During the war it became more and more difficult to obtain 'green' colours and so 'blues' were used instead. The handbook was reprinted in 1945 but the same card containing samples of the colours was retained. Great efforts were made to eliminate shadows by painting the area in shadow in a lighter colour. Deck fittings were normally painted lighter than their surrounds, again to minimise shadows.

For the lighter schemes (ie Western Approaches and Light and Intermediate Admiralty patterns) masts were generally painted white. Decks were generally B30 (Medium Blue-Green) for the former of these schemes, G20 (Medium Grey-Green) and G10 (Dark Grey-Green) for the other two and G5 (Extra Dark Grey-Green) for Dark Admiralty schemes. Where Corticene was used, it retained its normal colour, a mid-grey.

Before the Admiralty introduced their official schemes, the naturalist Peter Scott defined the Western Approaches scheme – mainly white with areas of light green and pale blue – and this was included in the official handbook. 'Mountbatten Pink' was popular with the ships of Mountbatten's own flotilla but was not well thought of by camouflage experts, particularly for operations around the times of sunset and sunrise. It was considered as maybe having some advantage for night operations when it often appeared darker than grey colours.

As radar developed, it nullified the effects of camouflage and so the emphasis changed to 'confusion' rather than 'concealment'. Towards the end of the war, most ships had changed to a much simpler pattern – overall grey with a darker (blue or grey) panel on the hull. For destroyers, these panels generally started level with the front of the forward turret muzzle and continued to the aft end of the superstructure.

White Ensign Models produce a range of paints (ColourCoats) which are closely matched to original paint chips but it is still necessary to make allowance for wear and tear (particularly in the rough waters of the North Atlantic) and fading (relevant in the Mediterranean and Pacific), as well as the much discussed (and disputed) 'scale effect'.

Wartime Operations

The majority of earlier fleet destroyers led very active lives during the Second World War, but some were not completed until just before the end of the war, or even later. Activities frequently involved escorting other ships, either merchant convoys or capital ships and aircraft carriers on major strikes and anti-submarine operations.

It was common practice during the war for the destroyers to 'work up' with the Home Fleet at Scapa Flow. This frequently resulted in the first vessel of a flotilla remaining there for a considerable period of time whilst others in the flotilla completed and also 'worked up' before the new flotilla was actually formed. They sometimes took part in Home Fleet operations, such as escorting convoys to Russia, during this period.

A number of both the 'J' and 'K' classes were involved in collisions during the early years of their service, frequently with other destroyers. This resulted in long periods being spent in refit or repair, as did machinery and structural defects, which were also common in these two classes. Many destroyers also experienced damage during rough weather, frequently requiring refits.

The evacuation of the British army from Dunkirk in France in May/June 1940 (Operation Dynamo) involved the vast majority of operational destroyers in home waters, and they suffered many casualties (six destroyers sunk and nineteen

damaged), *Jackal* being the only operational ship of her class at the end.

Some major actions involved fleet destroyers. HMS *Kimberley* was involved in the second battle of Narvik (June 1940), the only one of the modern fleet destroyers to be involved in either battle. Operating with the battleship HMS *Warspite*, the allied force sank three German destroyers and caused another five to be scuttled by their crews.

In November 1940 HMS *Jervis* and HMS *Janus* formed part of the fleet screen during air attacks on Italian warships at Taranto by aircraft from HMS *Illustrious* (Operation Judgement). Twenty-one Swordfish aircraft were launched in two waves: the first, of twelve aircraft, and the second, with nine aircraft. Some were armed with torpedoes, others with 250-pound bombs, and the flare aircraft each carried four bombs and sixteen flares. It was the first duty of the latter to lay the flares in a line so as to show

Above: HMS *Jervis* in 1939 appears very smart with pristine paintwork, something that will change rapidly when war begins. Her two sets of torpedo tubes and forward facing aft gun are clear to see. At this time she is not carrying a pennant number. *(National Museum of the Royal Navy)*

Below: HMS *Kipling* in July 1940. During this time she was receiving repairs to shock damage received during a high level bombing attack in April of that year. *(National Maritime Museum N11813)*

Above: The paintwork of HMS *Janus* shows significant signs of wear as she refuels form the battleship HMS *Valiant* during 1940/41. *(National Maritime Museum D1091)*

Below: Taken at the same time as the photo on page 2, HMS *Kandahar* is seen at Alexandria in 1941. The elaborate three-colour camouflage was unique to this ship and, in a slightly different pattern, her sisters *Kimberley* and *Kingston*. Colours were black, AP507B and AP507C. *(National Maritime Museum N31759)*

up in silhouette the Italian battleships in the outer harbour. When the last Swordfish attack was complete, Italy's serviceable battleships had been reduced from six to two – only *Vittorio Veneto* and *Giulio Cesare* had escaped damage – and all of this had been accomplished at the cost of only two Swordfish aircraft shot down.

In March 1941 HM Ships *Jervis*, *Jaguar* and *Janus* formed part of the screen for the larger ships during the battle of Cape Matapan. Following the action between the larger ships and the air attacks, destroyers took part in the night actions, the Italian cruiser *Zara* being sunk by a torpedo from HMS *Jervis* and *Pola* was eventually sunk by torpedoes from HM Ships *Jervis* and *Nubian*.

In November 1941 a boarding party from HMS *Onslow* captured the German Trawler *Fohn* and recovered an Enigma coding machine. HM Ships *Gurkha* (ex-*Larne*, renamed before launch), *Legion* and *Lightning* were involved in providing escort for the aircraft carriers flying-off aircraft to Malta, including that in the same month when *Ark Royal* was sunk during her return to Gibraltar, *Legion* embarking 1560 survivors.

The Mediterranean saw many actions involving destroyers, including the two battles of Sirte taking place in December 1941 and March 1942. HM Ships *Kimberley*, *Kingston*, *Kipling*, *Lance*, *Legion* and *Lively* were all involved in the first battle, an ineffectual skirmish which occurred when the Italians, escorting a convoy, spotted the British firing at aircraft and opened fire, withdrawing after just fifteen minutes as they wished to avoid a night engagement even though they had a superior force. *Kipling* did suffer one casualty from a near miss.

HM Ships *Jervis*, *Kipling*, *Kelvin*, *Kingston*, *Legion* and *Lively* were involved in the second battle when the British were escorting a convoy to Malta. Ranged against the British were a battleship, two heavy and one light cruiser and a number of destroyers. The battle raged for two and a half hours, with the British ships leaving the safety of their smoke screen to fire a few volleys and then returning to it when the Italian salvoes got too close. The destroyers launched torpedo attacks from about 5000yds but none of the torpedoes found their target. As *Kingston* turned she was hit by a round which penetrated her boiler room, ignited a fire and temporarily brought her to a halt. *Lively* was also struck by shell splinters from the battleship's main guns that pierced a bulkhead, causing some flooding but no casualties.

During August 1942 *Laforey*, *Quentin* and *Penn* took part in Operation Pedestal, a major effort to relieve Malta. This last was one of the destroyers to escort the crippled tanker *Ohio* when she finally arrived in Grand Harbour.

In December 1942 HMS *Onslow*'s commanding officer, Captain Sherbrooke, received a Victoria Cross for his gallant conduct during the battle of the Barents Sea. *Obdurate*, *Obedient* and *Orwell* were also present as part of the escort for the convoy JW51B. The German heavy cruisers

Admiral Hipper and *Lützow*, together with a number of destroyers, attacked the convoy, the British destroyers feigning a torpedo attack to deter them, and in a confused engagement *Admiral Hipper* hit *Onslow* causing heavy damage and many casualties including 17 killed. Although *Onslow* ultimately survived the action, Sherbrooke had been badly injured by a large steel splinter and command passed to HMS *Obedient*.

In December 1943 both *Matchless* and *Meteor* were involved in the engagement against the German battleship *Scharnhorst* (the battle of North Cape). With other destroyers, including the 'S' class *Scorpion*, *Savage*, HNorMS *Stord* (ex-HMS *Success*) and *Saumarez*, they attempted a torpedo attack against the damaged ship but, owing to extensive weather damage due to operations at high speed in the appalling conditions, HMS *Matchless* was unable to discharge her weapons. However, one torpedo from *Scorpion* and three from *Savage* found their mark and doomed the German ship.

The destroyers were involved in many landings (and evacuations) in Europe throughout the war, beginning with Norway and later moving on to North Africa (Operation Torch, November 1942), Italy (Operation Huskey, July 1943), Normandy, France (Operation Overlord, June 1944) and finally Southern France (Operation Dragoon, August 1944).

HMS *Saumarez*, present during the battle of North Cape, also led four of the 'V' class to take part in a classic destroyer action in May 1945 – the sinking of the Japanese cruiser *Haguro*. The 26th destroyer flotilla (*Saumarez, Verulam, Vigilant, Venus* and *Virago*), having been detached from TF 61, were in the Malacca Straits. The flotilla's only chance of success was if the enemy cruiser was intercepted at night as *Haguro* mounted ten 8in and eight 5in guns, easily outranging the guns mounted in the destroyers. At 2245 hours on 15 May *Venus* obtained a radar contact – the destroyers and the cruiser were on reciprocal courses. Captain (D), Captain M

Power in *Saumarez*, had his flotilla strung out in a semi-circle, into the centre of which the unsuspecting *Haguro* was steaming. Speed was reduced, and then the flotilla reversed course so that they were now on the same bearing as the cruiser. After some surprising manoeuvres by the Japanese, HMS *Saumarez* found herself on a collision course with *Haguro*'s consort, the destroyer *Kamikaze*. Fire was immediately opened on the destroyer and, after raking the *Kamikaze*, *Saumarez* turned her 4.7in guns on the *Haguro*. A single 8in hit on *Saumarez* clipped the top of her funnel, to be followed a few seconds later by a 5in hit amidships. The latter filled the engine room with steam, killing two men and bringing her to a halt but not before her full salvo of eight torpedoes had been launched; three, at least, struck *Haguro*. The other four destroyers meanwhile had come in to launch their torpedoes. First came *Verulam*, who launched her attack simultaneously with *Saumarez*; next *Venus*, who scored one hit, and *Virago*, who scored two, and last of all *Vigilant* with one more. After this *Venus*

came in again to deliver the coup de grace – two more torpedoes at point blank range – and *Haguro* sank at 0209 hrs on the 16th.

WARTIME LOSSES

'J' class

In May 1942 *Jackal* was deployed to intercept a convoy on passage to Benghazi. She came under heavy attack by German dive-bombers 60 miles north of Mersa Matruh and sustained major damage after a bomb hit which caused fires. She was taken in tow by *Jervis* but had to be abandoned when a fire in her boiler room became out of control. Survivors were taken off by *Jervis*, which sank the ship by torpedo.

In January 1942 *Jaguar* was escorting RFA *Slavok* when they came under attack by *U652*. She began to rescue survivors from the RFA, which had been set on fire aft by a torpedo and was herself hit by two torpedoes from the same submarine in a position north east of Sollum. She sank immediately with only 53 survivors; 193 of the ship's company lost their lives.

On 23 January 1944 *Janus* was hit by a torpedo during an air attack off Anzio and sank with heavy loss of life when a magazine exploded, 158 of the ship's company losing their lives.

On 2 May 1941, when entering Grand Harbour, Malta with ships of Force K after a fruitless search for convoys to and from Tripoli, *Jersey* detonated a mine laid in the entrance to the harbour by aircraft on the previous night. The ship sank blocking the entrance and no movements were possible for some days.

On 21 May 1941, whilst intercepting invasion craft on passage to Crete, *Juno* came under high level bombing attack by five CANT Z1007 aircraft and was hit by three bombs, which split the ship in two abaft the bridge structure, sinking her in less than two minutes; 96 of the crew were rescued by other destroyers.

Jupiter detonated a mine in position 6°45'S, 112°6'E on 27 February 1942. This occurred whilst with a multi-national Combined Striking Force attempting to

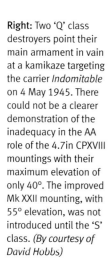

intercept the Japanese Eastern Invasion Force near Sourabaya. She remained afloat for four hours before sinking; 84 of the ships company were killed or missing, 97 were taken prisoner and 83 were either able to reach the shore or were rescued by the US Submarine *S38*. The minefield had been laid earlier that day by a Dutch minelayer without the knowledge of the Striking Force.

'K' class

Having been in the Mediterranean for just a month, on 23 May 1941 *Kelly* came under heavy air attacks by German aircraft south of Gavo, Crete, during which she was hit and sank within two minutes.

Kandahar was operating north of Tripoli when, on 19 December 1941, she sustained serious damage aft when she hit a mine whilst going to the aid of HMS *Neptune* which had also struck a mine. She was eventually sunk by torpedo from *Jaguar*, who rescued 174 men.

On 23 May 1941 *Kashmir* came under heavy air attacks by German aircraft during which she was hit and sank within two minutes south of Gavo, Crete. *Kashmir* had been operating with *Kelly* (which was also sunk) and *Kipling*, which rescued 159 survivors from *Kashmir*.

On 23 June 1940, whilst with *Kandahar* and *Kingston*, *Khartoum* suffered an explosion in an air vessel on the after torpedo tube mounting, possibly after being hit by fire from an Italian submarine. The explosion caused a serious uncontrollable fire which prevented access to magazine flooding controls and the resulting magazine explosion killed one of the ship's

company, injured three others and wrecked the stern structure aft of the engine room causing extensive flooding. The ship settled on an even keel with the forward structure awash. The ship's company were rescued by *Kandahar* and taken to Aden.

In April 1942 *Kingston* was declared a total constructive loss after being struck by bombs whilst in HM Dockyard, Malta. She was in dock for repairs following an engagement with a large force of Italian ships encountered whilst escorting convoy MW10 which was on passage from Alexandria to Malta.

On 11 April 1942 *Kipling* came under heavy air attacks by 14 Ju88 bombers based in Crete. She was hit during a second attack by aircraft based in Greece and sank quickly, 25 of the ships company losing their lives.

'L' class

Laforey spent much time in the Mediterranean but survived until 30 March 1944, when after several hours of depth charge attacks, *U223* surfaced and was engaged by surface gunfire from a number of ships, at a range of about 1500yds. Despite being hit repeatedly, *U223* fired three torpedoes which hit *Laforey* and quickly sank her, only 65 of the ship's company surviving out of a total of 247 on board.

On 5 April 1942 *Lance* was hit by a bomb whilst in dry dock for repairs at Malta. The wreck was later salved and towed to Chatham for a full survey, the result of which was that she was found to be beyond economical repair.

In January 1942, whilst acting as escort

Left: HMS *Jervis* at Malta in December 1945 shows the typical appearance of the survivors of the class at the end of the war. The lattice foremast carries Type 276 radar with a HF/DF aerial at the head of the topmast, while a light tripod mainmast carries the air search Type 291. Light AA armament comprises twin 20mm mountings in the bridge wings and two singles amidships on what had been the searchlight platform. The ship sports Admiralty Standard Scheme A designed for the British Pacific Fleet with a panel of B20 on G45; the funnel carries the black divisional leader's band and the flotilla number. *(A & J Pavia)*

Left: HMS *Legion* seen entering Grand Harbour Malta in December 1941. One of four 'L's completed with eight 4in guns instead of six 4.7s because of production bottlenecks with the large and complex Mk XX mountings, they were regarded as superior AA ships so were heavily used in the Mediterranean. Note she has a dark grey hull and light grey upperworks with three bands on her funnel. *(National Museum of the Royal Navy)*

Right: Just after the end of the war against Japan, *Penn* is seen as a unit of the British Pacific Fleet, where she was employed as an aircraft target to train aircrews. The ship has both sets of torpedo tubes, and all the 4in guns now have shields. Light AA includes a 40mm 'Boffin' mounting in the bridge wings and a single 20mm Oerlikon either side of the searchlight platform. Radar comprises the usual destroyer air-search set Type 291 at the masthead, but for surface search the ship has a US SG-1 on the fore top platform.

for convoy MW8B during its passage from Alexandria to Malta, *Larne* came under attack by *U133* west of Sollum and was hit by a torpedo. She caught fire and was surrounded by burning oil fuel but was towed clear by the Dutch destroyer *Isaac Sweers*, which was able to rescue all but nine of the ship's company before the ship sank in position 31°50'N, 29°14'E.

During March 1942, whilst escorting convoy MW10, *Legion* was damaged by a near miss whilst under air attack. On the 26th, whilst under repair in Malta, she was hit by two bombs during an air raid on Grand Harbour and sustained further serious damage. Her forward magazine exploded and she sank and rolled over with her bridge and funnel lying on the jetty.

Lightning operated off Bone during early 1943 and on 12 March she sailed from Bone with *Loyal* as screen for the cruisers *Aurora* and *Sirius* during a planned attack on a convoy on passage from Sicily to North Africa. The force came under schnellboot attack and *Lightning* was hit on the port side forward by a torpedo. This torpedo caused major damage and totally disabled the ship, and she was hit amidships soon afterwards by a second torpedo from the same craft, which inflicted tremendous damage, breaking the ship's back. *Lightning* sank quickly north of Bizerta

with the loss of 45 of the ship's company.

Loyal carried out a bombardment in the Cesebatico area on 11 October 1944, with *Lookout*. During the return passage the next day, she detonated a mine and sustained major structural damage to machinery which resulted in flooding. She was withdrawn from operational service and towed to Taranto where she remained until 1946.

'M' class

In February 1944, whilst escorting convoy JW57, *Mahratta* (ex-*Marksman*) came under U-boat attack and was hit by a T5 (FAT acoustic torpedo) fired by *U990* and sank quickly in the Barents Sea. Only 17 out of a total of over 217 in the ship's company were rescued.

Martin suffered a similar fate, being hit by three torpedoes and sunk by *U431*, 85 miles north east of Algiers on 10 November 1942 whilst escorting a military convoy during the build-up phase of Operation Torch, the landings in North Africa. Only 63 of the ship's company were rescued.

On 8 October 1943, ORP *Orkan* (ex-*Myrmidon*) came under attack by *U378* and was hit by an acoustic torpedo SW of Iceland. She sank within five minutes with heavy loss of life, only 44 of the ship's company being rescued.

Right: HMS *Virago* had the shorter version of the lattice mast, with Type 276 and the HF/DF aerial, but no pole mast aft, so no position for Type 291. She is seen as completed in October 1943 in an Admiralty Disruptive scheme. *(World Ship Society)*

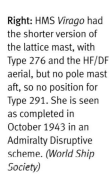

'N' class

In 1942 HMAS *Nestor* was part of the covering force for a convoy to Malta which came under heavy air attack, during which she sustained serious damage by three near misses, causing flooding of her boiler rooms. She was taken in tow by *Javelin* but on 16 June the tow broke and she was then sunk by *Javelin* using shallow set depth charges.

'P' class

In April 1943 *Pakenham* intercepted a convoy escorted by Italian torpedo boats south west of Marsala. Whilst sinking the escort *Cigno* with torpedoes after she had been disabled by surface gunfire, *Pakenham* was hit four times by return fire and sustained major damage which caused flooding in her engine room. She was taken in tow by *Paladin* but the tow had to be abandoned because of the threat of air attacks and *Pakenham* was sunk by a torpedo off Cape Granitola, the ship's company having been taken off by *Paladin*.

In October 1943, whilst bombarding shipping at Kalymos, *Panther* came under attack from dive bombers south of Scarpanto Strait. She received two direct hits and four near misses and quickly sank in position 35°48'N, 27°30'E.

In December 1942 *Partridge* was involved in an anti-submarine operation off Oran and was hit by a torpedo fired by *U565*. Both her engine and gearing rooms flooded causing the ship to break in two, in position 35°50'N, 01°35'W.

Pathfinder was damaged by air attack in February 1945 and declared a constructive total loss the following month.

In December 1942 *Porcupine* was hit by a torpedo fired by *U602*. She was towed back to Great Britain in two sections, which were then used for the accommodation of crews of landing craft in Stokes Bay at Portsmouth, being identified as Pork (Forward Section) and Pine (After Section).

'Q' class

In November 1943, whilst on Adriatic deployment, *Quail* struck a mine in the barrage laid by *U453* off Bari. She was

beached, moved to Taranto for repairs but capsized and sank in the Gulf of Taranto whilst on tow to Malta for permanent repair.

In December 1942 *Quentin* was in action with ships of Force Q against a convoy of four ships north of Cape Bon when she came under air attack during the return passage and was sunk by torpedo off Galita Island.

'S' class

During the Normandy landings, HNorMS *Svenner* (ex-*Shark*) was waiting off Sword beach for minesweepers to provide a swept channel for the bombarding ships when she came under attack by three S-boats and was hit by a torpedo amidships which broke her back.

On 24 June 1944 *Swift* detonated a mine off Sword beachhead during the Normandy landings and sank after breaking in two.

'V' class

In January 1944, *Hardy* sank after being hit by an acoustic Gnat torpedo (T5) fired

Above: There is a wealth of detail to be seen in this 1945 view of HMS *Wager* carrying out mail transfer with the carrier HMS *Victorious*. Although the barrels are under canvas, the AA mounts still carry twin 20mm Oerlikons, later to be replaced by single 40mm barrels, making them 'Boffins'; at the same time the searchlight was replaced by a single MkIII Bofors. *(National Museum of the Royal Navy)*

Left: *Whelp* in April 1944 as completed. She and *Wessex* carried a quad pom-pom amidships in lieu of the twin Hazemeyer Bofors which was in short supply. With her sisters of the 27th Destroyer Flotilla, she was sent to join the newly constituted British Pacific Fleet in January 1945.*(By courtesy of David Hobbs)*

Above: HMS *Barfleur* was the first 'Battle' to complete, in September 1944, and was painted with camouflage ready for war. She was the only one of the class to see action, although *Armada*, *Camperdown*, *Hogue* and *Trafalgar* were assigned to the British Pacific Fleet before the Japanese surrender.

by *U278* during defence of convoy JW56B (her third convoy) against enemy submarine attacks.

POSTWAR

At the end of the Second World War there was a pressing need for high speed anti-submarine ships. There was also a surplus of destroyers, the majority of which had the speed capability and had experienced relatively short service careers.

In the 1950s a total of 23 destroyers underwent 'full conversion' to Type 15 frigates for the Royal Navy. These conversions involved vastly increasing the size of the superstructure, hence the use of large amounts of aluminium to minimise top weight, and the installation of two three barrelled ahead-throwing ASW mortars, either Squid or, when available, the Mk 10 Limbo. The conversions were expensive and so another ten destroyers underwent more limited conversion to Type 16 frigates during which they received two Squid ASW mortars but retained their 'destroyer' appearance.

These ships all came from the 'Emergency' destroyer classes (mainly the 'R', 'T' and 'U' classes), the majority of the 'C' class and all the 'Battle' class continuing to serve in the Royal Navy as fleet destroyers, four of the 'Battle' class subsequently being converted to radar pickets. Other surviving vessels were sold to numerous countries, including Turkey, Pakistan and the Netherlands, where they continued to serve for many years.

Of all the destroyers built during the war, only one survives in the United Kingdom. *Cavalier* is preserved as a museum ship and is on display at the Chatham Historic Dockyard.

HMS *Kelvin* 1939

All drawings are reproduced at 1:700 scale

HMS *Lance* 1941

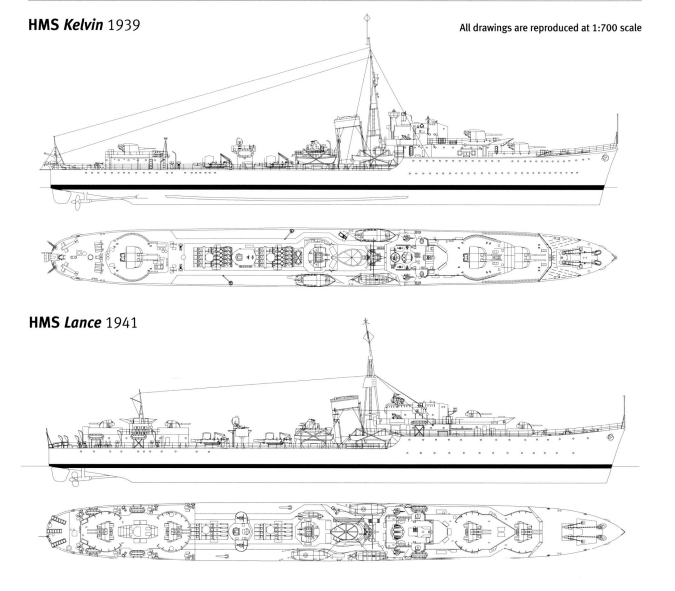

HMS *Milne* 1942

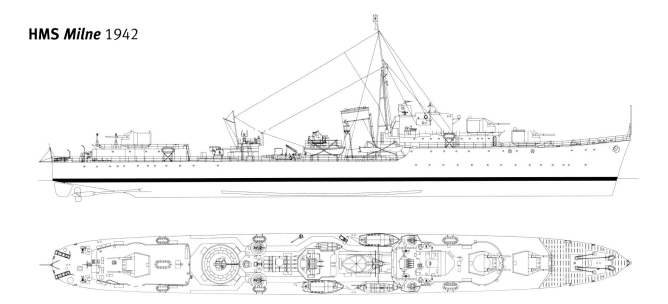

HMS *Napier* 1940

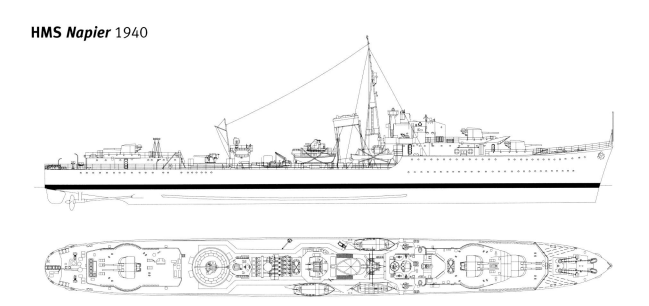

HMS *Napier* 1942

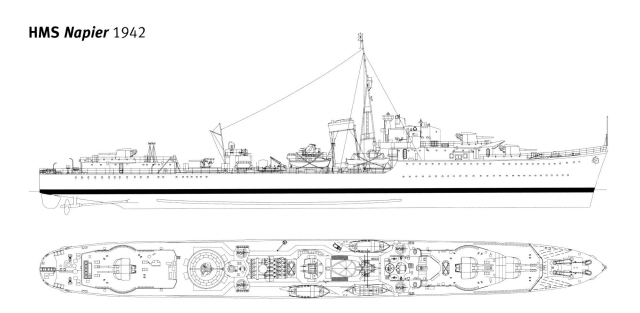

HMS *Onslow* 1941

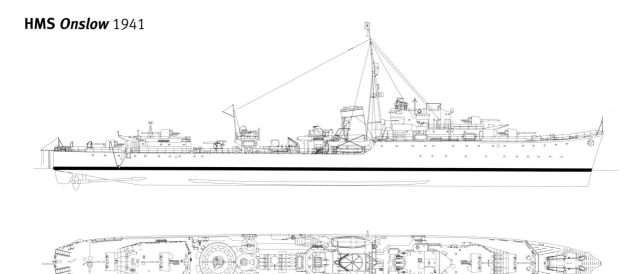

HMS *Obedient* 1942

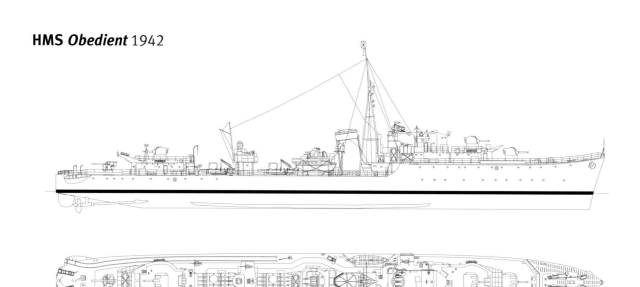

HMS *Scorpion* 1943

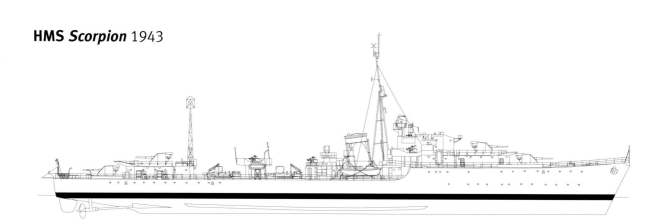

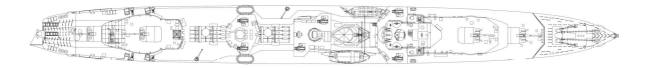

HMS *Savage* 1944

HMS *Caesar* 1944

HMS *Barfleur* 1944

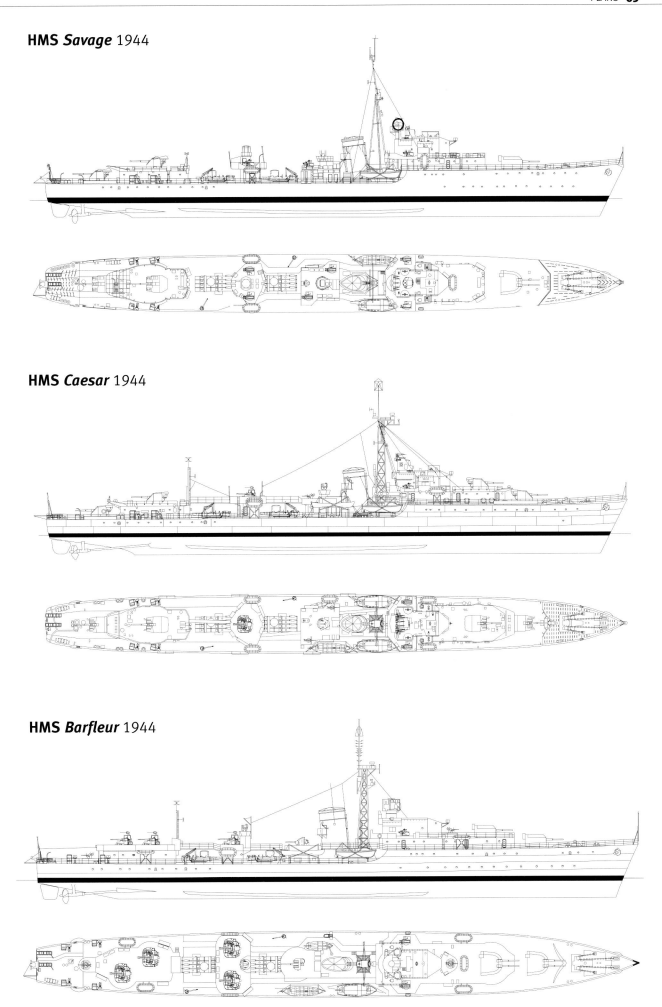

Selected References

BOOKS

Afridi To Nizam: British Fleet Destroyers 1937-43, John English (World Ship Society 2001)

British and Empire Warships of the Second World War, H T Lenton (Greenhill Books 1998)

British Destroyers, 1892-1953, Edgar J March (Seeley Service & Co Ltd 1966)

British Destroyers & Frigates: The Second World War And After, Norman Friedman (Chatham Publishing 2006)

Conway's All The World's Fighting Ships, 1922-1946, edited by Roger Chesneau (Conway Maritime Press Ltd 1980)

Destroyers of World War Two, M J Whitley (Arms and Armour Press 1988)

Destroyer Weapons of World War 2, Peter Hodges and Norman Friedman (Conway Maritime Press 1979)

Ensign 6: War Built Destroyers, O To Z Classes, Alan Raven and John Roberts (Bivouac Books Ltd 1976)

Naval Camouflage 1914-1945, David Williams (Chatham Publishing 2001)

Obdurate To Daring: British Fleet Destroyers 1941-1945, John English (World Ship Society 2008)

Royal Navy Destroyers, 1893 to the Present Day, Maurice Cocker (The History Press 2011)

The British Destroyer, T D Manning (Putnam & Co Ltd 1961)

The Kelly's: British J, K & N Class Destroyers of World War II, Christopher Langtree (Chatham Publishing 2002)

Waterline Warships: An Illustrated Masterclass, Philip Reed (Seaforth Publishing 2010)

MODEL MANUFACTURERS

ADMIRALTY MODEL WORKS
14269 Lagoon Cove Lane, Winter Garden, FL, 34787-5937, USA
www.admiraltymodelworks.com

APS MODELS
PO Box 5025, Gwandalan, NSW 2259, Australia

COMMANDER SERIES MODELS, INC
551 Wegman Road, Rochester, NY 14624, USA
www.commanderseries.com

DEAN'S MARINE
Conquest Drove, Farcet Fen, Peterborough, PE7 3DH, UK. www.deansmmarine.co.uk

EDUARD MODEL-ACCESSORIES
Mírová 170, 43521 Obrnice, Czech Republic
www.eduard.cz

FLEETSCALE
Westward Mouldings Ltd, The New Factory, Greenhill, Delaware Road, Gunnislake, Cornwall, PL18 9AS, UK
www.fleetscale.com

GHQ MODELS
28100 Woodside Road, Shorewood, MN 55331-2693, USA.
www.ghqmodels.com

GOLD MEDAL MODELS
PO Box 670, Lopez, WA 98261, USA
http://goldmm.com/

HP MODELS
Postfach 101151, 46471 Wesel, Germany
www.hp-models.com

JOHN R HAYNES
Fallowden Farm, Ashdon, Saffron Walden, Essex, CB10 2HL, UK. www.johnrhaynes.com

L'ARSENAL
Boîte Postal No2, 14790 Verson, France
www.larsenal.com

MARCLE MODELS
Turnagain, Finch Lane, Amersham, Buckinghamshire, HP7 9NE, UK. www.marcle.co.uk

METCALF MOULDINGS
1 Wentworth Cottages, Haultwick, Dane End, Nr Ware, Herts, SG11 1JG, UK. http://business.virgin.net/metcalf.mouldings/catalogue.htm

MOLE MARITIME MODELS
c/o Dorking Models, 12-13 West Street, Dorking, Surrey, RH4 1BL, UK. www.dorkingmodels.com

MOUNTFORD METAL MINIATURES LTD.
14 Cherry Tree Drive, Duckmanton, Chesterfield, S44 5JL, UK. www.mountfordminiatures.com

NAVIS MODELLBAU
Dr. I. Kraus, Mozartweg 2, D-82538 Geretsried, Germany. www.navis-neptun.de

NIKO MODEL
ul. Gombrowicza 39/32, 59-220 Legnica, Poland
www.nikomdel.pl

QUAYCRAFT
73 Chambercombe Road, Ilfracombe, North Devon, EX34 9PH, UK. www.quaycraft.co.uk

SKYTREX LIMITED
Unit 1, Charnwood Business Park, North Road, Loughborough, LE11 1LE, UK. www.skytrex.com

SUPERIOR MODELS
PO Box 10, Belle Haven, VA 23306, USA
www.alnavco.com

TAMIYA Inc
3-7 Ondawara, Suruga-Kll, Schizuoka 422-8610, Japan. www.tamiya.com

TOM'S MODELWORKS
PO Box 304, Santa Rosa, CA 95402, USA
www.tomsmodelworks.com

WHITE ENSIGN MODELS LTD
Unit 5, Cobnash Industrial Estate, Kingsland, Leominster, HR6 9RW, UK
www.whiteensignmodels.com